Pain and Gain

Implementing No Child Left Behind in Three States, 2004–2006

Brian M. Stecher, Scott Epstein, Laura S. Hamilton,

Julie A. Marsh, Abby Robyn, Jennifer Sloan McCombs,

Jennifer Russell, Scott Naftel

Sponsored by the National Science Foundation

 EDUCATION

The research described in this report was sponsored by the National Science Foundation and was conducted by RAND Education, a unit of the RAND Corporation.

Library of Congress Cataloging-in-Publication Data is available for this publication.

ISBN: 978-0-8330-4610-9

Published 2008 by the RAND Corporation
1776 Main Street, P.O. Box 2138, Santa Monica, CA 90407-2138
1200 South Hayes Street, Arlington, VA 22202-5050
4570 Fifth Avenue, Suite 600, Pittsburgh, PA 15213-2665
RAND URL: http://www.rand.org/
To order RAND documents or to obtain additional information, contact
Distribution Services: Telephone: (310) 451-7002;
Fax: (310) 451-6915; Email: order@rand.org

Preface

The Implementing Standards-Based Accountability (ISBA) study was designed to examine the strategies that states, districts, and schools are using to implement standards-based accountability (SBA) under the No Child Left Behind Act (NCLB) and how these strategies are associated with classroom practices and student achievement in mathematics and science. This monograph presents the final results of the ISBA project. It contains descriptive information regarding the implementation of NCLB in California, Georgia, and Pennsylvania from 2003–2004 through 2005–2006. It is a companion to MG-589-NSF, *Standards-Based Accountability Under No Child Left Behind* (2007), and updates those findings with an additional year of data, permitting further analyses of state-to-state differences and longer-term trends. Like the companion report, this monograph should be of particular interest to educators and policymakers in California, Georgia, and Pennsylvania, and of general interest to those concerned with standards-based reforms and NCLB.

This study suggests that school improvement efforts might be more effective if they were responsive to local conditions and customized to address the specific causes of failure and the capacity of the school in question.

This research was conducted by RAND Education, a unit of the RAND Corporation. It is part of a larger body of work addressing accountability in state and federal education. The project was sponsored by the National Science Foundation. Any opinions, findings, conclusions, or recommendations expressed in this monograph are those of the authors and do not necessarily reflect the views of the National Science Foundation.

Contents

Figures

Tables

Summary

NCLB, perhaps the most significant federal policy relating to K–12 public education, requires each state to create a standards-based accountability system that includes three components: (1) academic standards, (2) assessments to measure student mastery of the standards, and (3) consequences to encourage improved performance. NCLB makes significant demands on states, districts, and schools. However, the law also gives educators a great deal of flexibility in how they reach NCLB goals. The success of NCLB is therefore partially dependent on how districts and schools implement the law and what policies and strategies these entities rely on to improve student achievement.

The ISBA study was designed to examine what strategies states, districts, and schools are using to implement SBA and how these strategies are associated with classroom practices and student achievement in mathematics and science. The ISBA study was structured as a set of three state-specific case studies; we collected longitudinal data from California, Georgia, and Pennsylvania each year for three years from the 2003–2004 school year through the 2005–2006 school year. This monograph is an update of *Standards-Based Accountability Under No Child Left Behind* (Hamilton et al., 2007), which was based on data from the 2003–2004 and 2004–2005 school years of data collection.

The companion monograph contained detailed information about the attitudes and actions of superintendents, principals, and teachers in each of the states, and it drew a number of general conclusions. In that monograph, we found that the accountability systems enacted in response to NCLB differed in important ways across the three states, including the content of their academic standards, the difficulty of their performance standards, and their systems for support and technical assistance. Despite these differences, districts and schools responded to the accountability systems in broadly similar ways. For example, principals reported similar school improvement efforts focusing on aligning standards, curriculum, and assessments; providing extra instruction to low-performing students; and using test results for instructional planning. Teachers enacted these initiatives in their classrooms and generally felt the changes benefited students. However, teachers also reported narrowing the curriculum toward tested topics and focusing on students near the proficient cutoff score, and some complained of lowered morale among their peers and lack of alignment between tested goals and their local curriculum materials. Administrators were generally more positive toward the reform than teachers, but both identified similar factors that hindered their efforts to improve student performance. These hindrances included inadequate resources and lack of instructional time, but they also included students' lack of basic skills and inadequate support from parents. We recommended strengthened efforts to align system components, development of teacher and administrator capacities for improvement, and the development of better methods for measuring school and student performance.

For the most part, those findings and recommendations still hold. However, the additional year of data collected in 2006 enabled us to refine the analyses, particularly examining more carefully state-to-state variations and multiyear trends. In this monograph, we draw upon superintendent, principal, and teacher survey data from all three years of our data collection to explore the further development of policies and practices in each of the three states. For each state, we address the following four basic research questions:

1. How did districts, schools, and teachers respond to state accountability efforts, including state standards and state tests?
2. What school improvement strategies were used and which were perceived to be most useful?
3. What was the impact of accountability on curriculum, teacher practice, and student learning?
4. What conditions hindered district, school, and teacher improvement efforts?

Study Methods

We chose California, Georgia, and Pennsylvania because of their diversity in terms of geography, demography, and their approaches to implementing NCLB. The study used a combination of large-scale, quantitative data collection and small-scale case study methods to examine NCLB implementation at the state, district, school, and classroom levels. At the state level, we conducted interviews with key stakeholders and collected relevant documents. District-level data were collected from superintendents through paper-and-pencil surveys in each year and through semistructured telephone interviews in the first and third years. School-level data were gathered each year through principal and teacher surveys and through annual case studies in a small subsample of schools.

We selected a random sample of districts stratified by size, and we randomly selected "regular" elementary and middle schools (excluding charter schools, alternative schools, and the like) from the districts that agreed to cooperate. In participating elementary schools, we administered surveys to all teachers who taught math and science in grades three, four, and five, and in participating middle schools, we administered surveys to all teachers who taught these subjects in grades seven and eight.

Response rates were quite high for each of the three surveys (superintendent, principal, and teacher) each year (see Tables A.5 and A.6). To analyze survey responses, we generated sampling and nonresponse weights for each state. Using these weights, we are able to report statewide estimates of the responses of superintendents, principals, and teachers from regular public schools and districts.

Findings

We structured the ISBA study as a set of three parallel case studies in different contexts, and we found that state context affected the implementation of NCLB. As a result, we report findings in separate chapters for each state. Nevertheless, there were some common themes across the three states, and these findings are largely consistent with large-scale studies of the implementation of NCLB (U.S. Department of Education, 2007a and 2007b; Center on Education Policy [CEP], 2006, 2007a, 2007b, and 2008).

Common Themes Across States

By the end of this study, all three states had constructed most of the infrastructure needed to support standards-based accountability (standards, assessments, reporting structures), and most educators understood the reforms. At all levels of the education hierarchy, alignment among standards, assessments, and curriculum was a major focus of NCLB implementation. However, despite these efforts, there were still concerns about misalignment, especially among teachers.

Educators generally reported that they found test data useful for teaching, particularly data from progress tests that were an increasingly widespread tool in the three states.[1] Educators reported a variety of positive effects of accountability, including improvements in academic rigor, instruction, and focus on student learning. Administrators were generally more positive about the effects of NCLB than teachers. Despite the fact that many teachers reported that accountability had improved learning, they were more likely to question the validity of state test results, and a majority of teachers did not believe the system was beneficial for students. Teachers were concerned with many aspects of NCLB. Some teachers were worried that the standards were too difficult for certain students, and at the same time some teachers were concerned that the curriculum was not challenging enough for high-achieving students.

Districts and schools engaged in a wide variety of reforms, including improving alignment of curriculum and instruction to standards and assessments, using data

---

[1] Progress tests are formal assessments given periodically during the year to measure student progress in mastering state standards. They are also called interim tests, formative tests, and benchmark tests. To our knowledge, the outcomes of these exams do not result in any consequences for teachers in the districts we studied.

to improve instruction, and focusing on low-performing students. Some changes in practice, such as the adoption of progress tests, have occurred more rapidly or more completely in elementary schools than in middle schools. As expected, given NCLB's focus on math and reading, far more effort has been made to implement standards-based accountability in mathematics than in science. Many administrators indicated that their efforts to improve school performance were hindered by lack of funding and lack of time. Many teachers said their efforts to improve student performance were hindered by lack of time, large and heterogeneous classes, and poor student preparation.

Trends

Over the three years, each of the states made progress ironing out the kinks in its accountability systems. For example, test results were provided more quickly or in more diverse ways. Also, during this time period, educators' responses about the effects of NCLB became more positive; greater proportions of educators reported that accountability had improved academic rigor and focus on student learning. Concerns about the effects of NCLB on teacher morale continued, but the prevalence of these concerns decreased over time.

State-Specific Findings

Generally, educators in Georgia reported more-positive attitudes toward SBA than educators in California and Pennsylvania. This difference could be due to lower proficiency standards in the state that make it easier for students to reach proficiency and for schools to make AYP and avoid NCLB interventions, better implementation, or other state contextual factors, such as the lack of a strong union presence in Georgia. Pennsylvania educators generally had more negative attitudes toward SBA, perhaps because of the state's long tradition of local control over schools, or perhaps because of more-limited capacity on the part of the Pennsylvania Department of Education to offer support and assistance.

The Future of NCLB

This study suggests that NCLB has led to distinctive accountability systems in each state—different standards, different assessments, different support and assistance strategies—although each was derived from the same federal legislation and has the same set of consequences. The reauthorization of the Elementary and Secondary Education Act should recognize that this variation exists and develop policies accordingly. In some cases, new regulations may be needed to reduce or eliminate differences—e.g., to make proficiency in reading and mathematics similar across states. This study found a number of attitudes and behaviors associated with the overall level of student proficiency in the states. In other cases, it may be appropriate to relax rules to give states additional flexibility. This study suggests that school improvement efforts might be more effective if they were responsive to local conditions. Rather than imposing a fixed set of choices that apply when schools fail to achieve AYP for a given number of years, improvement efforts should be customized to address the specific causes of the failure and the capacity that exists locally.

There is also a lesson for SBA in general. Educators have become comfortable with the underlying SBA theory of action—set clear goals, develop measures, and establish consequences to encourage educators to achieve them. They are not comfortable when the implementation of that theory seems inconsistent with their local situation—e.g., when the standards do not match their local curriculum, when the proficient level seems unattainable for many of their students, or when their school is judged against targets that feel unattainable. It would seem that engaging educators in the development or refinement of the SBA framework (e.g., the reauthorization of NCLB) would be a good way to attempt to bridge this gap.

Acknowledgments

A large number of people contributed to the success of the ISBA project, and we want to acknowledge their efforts. The extensive survey data collection was handled with skill and efficiency by Timothy Smith, Debbie Alexander, and the staff of Westat, Inc. Thoughtful suggestions regarding the project were provided by our advisory committee, consisting of Philip Daro, Geno Flores, Adam Gamoran, Margaret Goertz, Clara Keith, Edys Quellmalz, and Carina Wong. We are also grateful to the staff of the California, Georgia, and Pennsylvania departments of education, who spoke with us and gave us access to information, and to the dozens of superintendents, hundreds of principals, and thousands of teachers who responded to our surveys and interviews each year. A number of RAND staff contributed to data collection and analysis in previous years, and their contribution was acknowledged in the companion report. Donna White provided continuing assistance throughout the project. Finally, we want to thank Diane Stark Renter of the Center on Education Policy and Georges Vernez of RAND for their thoughtful reviews of this monograph; their comments helped us improve both the organization and the presentation of this document.

Abbreviations

AMO	annual measurable objective
API	academic performance index
Avlb	Available
AYP	adequate yearly progress
CEP	Center on Education Policy
CST	California Standards Test
ELA	English language arts
Elem	elementary school
ELL	English language learner
ESEA	Elementary and Secondary Education Act
GPS	Georgia Performance Standards
HPSGP	High Priority Schools Grant Program
IEP	individualized education program
II/USP	Immediate Intervention/Underperforming Schools Program
ISBA	Implementing Standards-Based Accountability
LEP	limited English proficiency
MAP	Measures of Academic Progress
Mid	middle school
NA	not applicable
NAEP	National Assessment of Educational Progress

NCES	National Center for Education Statistics
NCLB	No Child Left Behind Act
PD	professional development
PPI	Pennsylvania Performance Index
PSAA	Public School Accountability Act of 1999
PSSA	Pennsylvania System of School Assessment
QCC	Quality Core Curriculum
SBA	standards-based accountability
Sci	science
SE	standard error
SSAS	state single accountability system
Usfl	useful

CHAPTER ONE

Introduction and Methods

The No Child Left Behind (NCLB) Act of 2001 (20 U.S.C. § 6311 et seq.) is currently the preeminent federal policy relating to K–12 public education, and at its center are its standards-based accountability (SBA) provisions. NCLB requires that each state create an SBA system that includes three main components: (1) academic standards, (2) assessments to measure student mastery of the standards, and (3) incentives to improve performance. In the case of NCLB, the incentives take the form of a series of interventions and sanctions for schools and districts whose students fail to demonstrate mastery on the assessments. The Implementing Standards-Based Accountability (ISBA) study was designed to examine what strategies states, districts, and schools are using to implement SBA under NCLB and how these strategies are associated with classroom practice and student achievement in mathematics and science. The ISBA study was designed as a set of three state-specific case studies; we collected data from California, Georgia, and Pennsylvania longitudinally from the 2003–2004 school year through the 2005–2006 school year.

This monograph is an update of *Standards-Based Accountability Under No Child Left Behind* (Hamilton et al., 2007), which reported on data from the 2003–2004 and 2004–2005 years of data collection. The companion monograph presented descriptive results relating to educators' attitudes toward SBA, district and school improvement strategies, changes in classroom practices, and perceived barriers to improvement.

Findings from the Previous Monograph

- *State accountability systems enacted in response to NCLB differed across the three states.*

  The three state systems differed with respect to the content of the academic standards, the difficulty level of their performance standards, their choice of additional indicators, and their school and district support and technical assistance mechanisms, just to name a few areas. Many of the differences were related to pre-NCLB contextual factors, including the degree to which the state had already been engaged in SBA efforts prior to NCLB.

- *Districts and schools responded to the new state accountability systems actively and in broadly similar ways, despite state differences.*

In all three states, majorities of school and district administrators described similar types of school-improvement activities, including aligning curricula with standards, providing technical assistance to help schools improve, and offering a variety of professional development (PD) opportunities for principals and teachers. Principals reported providing extra learning opportunities for low-performing students, promoting the use of student test results for instructional planning, implementing test preparation activities, and adopting interim or progress tests to provide more frequent assessment information. Georgia districts and schools were especially active in promoting science instruction and in adopting interim assessment systems compared with districts or schools in California and Pennsylvania.

- *Reported changes at the classroom level included both desirable and undesirable responses.*

On the positive side, teachers reported efforts to align instruction with standards and efforts to improve their own practices. On the negative side, teachers reported narrowing of curriculum and instruction toward tested topics and even toward certain problem styles or formats and focusing more on students near the proficient cutoff score (i.e., bubble kids), which, they said, might have negative effects on the learning opportunities given to high-achieving students.

- *Educators expressed support for NCLB goals but had concerns about specific features and effects.*

For instance, most administrators thought that state test scores accurately reflected student achievement, a sentiment that only a small minority of teachers shared. Teachers were particularly attuned to lack of consistency between state accountability requirements and local resources and programs. Teachers associated the implementation of SBA with reduced morale and expressed concerns about negative effects on their teaching.

- *Several perceived hindrances may stand in the way of effective implementation of NCLB.*

Most administrators thought that inadequate funding was hampering their school-improvement efforts, and many said that they did not have adequate numbers of highly qualified teachers in mathematics or science. Administrators and teachers alike saw insufficient instructional time and insufficient planning time as barriers. In addition, teachers reported that students' lack of basic skills, inadequate support from parents, and student absenteeism and tardiness hampered their efforts.

We drew four implications from these results: (1) alignment efforts at all levels need to be improved, (2) teacher and administrator capacity for school improvement needs to be enhanced, (3) better measures of school and student performance need to be developed, and (4) teacher concerns about negative consequences need to be addressed. Despite substantial state-to-state differences in the specific features of each accountability system, it appears that NCLB's single-minded emphasis on student proficiency on tests has both heightened schools' focus on outcomes and led to potentially negative consequences. One of the key challenges facing educators is to identify ways to increase the prevalence of desirable responses and minimize the undesirable ones, given the context in which educators are working.

The Current Study

This monograph builds on the companion document by presenting results from all three years of the ISBA study and examining trends across time in each of the states. Presenting results separately by state allows us to focus on the unique experience of each state in implementing SBA over the three-year period. Cross-state comparisons can also be illuminating; thus, we report on important differences among the states within the state-specific sections. For each state, we address the following four basic research questions:

1. How did districts, schools, and teachers respond to state accountability efforts, including state standards and state tests?
2. What school improvement strategies were used and which were perceived to be most useful?
3. What was the impact of accountability on curriculum, teacher practice, and student learning?
4. What conditions hindered district, school, and teacher improvement efforts?

In most cases, responses within a state were consistent across the three years, although there are important examples of areas where responses evolved over time, which we highlight. We also considered how responses varied across school level (elementary school versus middle school), subject (mathematics versus science), and the administrative hierarchy (teachers, principals, and superintendents).

Overview of Standards-Based Accountability Under No Child Left Behind

In theory, the three components of SBA (standards, assessments, and consequences) form a coherent system that focuses on improving student achievement. Standards describe what content students should be learning and the level of mastery students should be able to demonstrate. In addition, the standards are expected to serve both as a basis for the creation of assessments and as a guide for educators' curriculum development and instruction. The assessments measure how well students have mastered the skills and knowledge contained in the standards, and aggregate test scores serve as an indicator of schools' success in making sure children learn. Consequences for schools might include rewards for those whose students perform well and assistance and/or sanctions for those whose students do not. Essentially, the system creates a feedback loop that is intended to give educators the data and incentives necessary to improve educational practice and consequently increase student achievement.

SBA systems can be structured in many different ways. Under NCLB, for example, the incentives structure is multifaceted. Schools that do not meet performance expectations are first given extra support in the form of improvement planning and PD, and only later are sanctions applied.[1] In addition, students within those schools are given options to receive supplemental tutoring or to transfer to another school. These options, while potentially beneficial to individual students, also act as indirect incentives to schools and districts because of their effects on how funds must be allocated.

NCLB requires each state to create an SBA system with seven basic components:

- Academic content standards in reading, mathematics, and science indicate what students should know and be able to do.
- Annual assessments are aligned with the academic content standards in reading and mathematics in grades three through eight and once in high school and, in science, once in elementary school, once in middle school, and once in high school.
- Achievement standards for reading, mathematics, and science indicate the level of test performance that corresponds to "proficient" and other levels of performance (sometimes called performance standards).
- Annual measurable objectives (AMOs) in reading and mathematics indicate the percentage of students who are expected to be proficient each year, which increases annually until all students reach proficiency in 2014. AMOs are applied to all students (i.e., to the school and to the district as a whole) and to designated subgroups, including students from major racial and ethnic groups, low-income

---

[1]   A more complete explanation of the stages of interventions can be found in U.S. Department of Education (2007b).

students, students with limited English proficiency (LEP), and students with disabilities (if each group is of sufficient size).[2]

- There is an additional academic indicator chosen by the state. (For high schools, this indicator must be the graduation rate, but each state can select its own indicators for other levels.)
- Adequate yearly progress (AYP) calculations for schools and districts indicate whether all students and all significant subgroups of students have reached AMOs in reading and mathematics and whether the school made progress on the additional academic indicator (a school or district makes AYP only if it meets all the requirements for all subgroups).
- There are interventions and sanctions for Title I[3] schools and districts that do not make AYP for two or more years. After two years, the mandatory interventions include formal planning for improvement, PD, and the requirement that schools offer parents the opportunity to transfer their child to a school that is not low performing (with transportation provided). After three consecutive years of not making AYP, schools must also offer students supplemental educational services (i.e., tutoring). The interventions escalate in subsequent years to staffing changes and major governance changes, such as state takeover or reconstitution as a charter school.

As the above list demonstrates, NCLB makes significant demands on states, districts, and schools. However, the law also gives educators a great deal of flexibility in how they reach NCLB goals. Each state designs its own content standards, assessments, and performance standards. Although all students are expected to be proficient by 2014, states decide the interim targets. Perhaps most significantly, other than dictating certain interventions for failing schools, NCLB does not tell schools how to make the achievement gains that are needed to meet escalating performance targets nor what their policies should be for subjects that are not included in the accountability computations, such as social studies, science, art, or music. The success of NCLB is therefore largely dependent on how districts and schools implement the law and what policies and strategies these entities rely on to improve student achievement.

---

[2]   The science test results must be made public, but there are no annual measurable objectives for science, and science performance does count in calculating a school's adequate yearly progress, which is described below.

[3]   Title I is the first section of the Elementary and Secondary Education Act (ESEA), which NCLB reauthorized. Title I provides federal funds to schools providing education to low-income students.

Study Approach and Methods

Sampling

The three states we chose to study were selected to provide diversity in terms of geography, demography, and their approaches to implementing NCLB (see Tables A.1 and A.2). California is the largest of the states with over 6.4 million students in 2005–2006 and has the most diverse student population. It is the only state of the three with a large population of English language learners (about one-quarter of the student population in 2005–2006) and has much larger populations of Hispanic and Asian students than the other states (47 percent and 11 percent of the student population, respectively). Georgia has the largest proportion of African American students (38 percent in 2005–2006). Pennsylvania is the least diverse of the states and has the lowest percentage of economically disadvantaged students; less than a third of Pennsylvania students were eligible for free or reduced-price lunches in 2005–2006, as compared with about half of students in California and Georgia. Of the three states, California had the most complete SBA system prior to the enactment of NCLB. Georgia had just started to implement an SBA system when NCLB was enacted and therefore had the smoothest transition to NCLB compliance. Pennsylvania had a strong tradition of local control and, therefore, had to work more quickly than the other states to develop the standards, assessments, and accountability polices that NCLB requires.

In the first year of our data collection (2003–2004), we selected an initial sample of 27 districts in each state. Districts in each state were stratified based on the number of elementary and middle schools, and a random sample was drawn within each stratum. We were not able to recruit as many districts as we had hoped for and, therefore, drew a supplemental sample of 23 districts. The total sample for the first year was 104 districts, 68 of which agreed to participate in the study, representing a cooperation rate of 65 percent. In 2004–2005, we selected an additional supplemental sample of 28 districts in order to yield greater analytic power and to increase the number of districts with high percentages of schools struggling to meet NCLB requirements. This increased the total sample to 132 districts, 92 of which agreed to participate in the 2004–2005 year of the study. All 92 of these districts agreed to continue with the study for the 2005–2006 year of data collection (see Table A.3).

The school sample was restricted to include only "regular" public schools; charter schools, alternative schools, vocational schools, special education schools, and small schools were all excluded. In 2003–2004, 297 schools were randomly selected from the cooperating districts. The number of schools sampled in each district was based on district size and ranged from one to five elementary schools, and one to five middle schools. Of these schools, 267 agreed to participate in 2003–2004, representing a cooperation rate of 90 percent. The participating schools were contacted again in 2004–2005, as well as additional schools from the supplemental sample of districts. The total sample for 2004–2005 was 353 schools, 301 of which participated, representing a cooperation rate of 85 percent. In 2005–2006, two schools in Pennsylvania dropped out of the study, decreasing the cooperation rate by approximately 0.5 percent (see Table A.4). Most of the schools in the sample made AYP each year of the study, but the rates were different across the states. For example, in 2006, 61 percent of the sampled schools in California, 76 percent of the sampled schools in Georgia, and 83 percent of the sampled schools in Pennsylvania made AYP, according to principal reports. Principals also reported that only a small fraction of the schools in the sample were identified for improvement: 15, 23, and 10 percent, respectively, in California, Georgia, and Pennsylvania.

Each year, we asked cooperating elementary schools for a roster of teachers who taught math and science in grades three, four, and five, and we asked middle schools for a roster of teachers who taught these subjects in grades seven and eight. We administered surveys to all of those teachers. Each annual teacher sample was drawn independently; we did not track teachers over time. Over 3,000 teachers were surveyed each year.

Data Collection

At the state level, we conducted semistructured face-to-face interviews with a variety of key stakeholders, including high-level state department of education officials, legislators and legislative staff, state board of education staff, and union and state school boards' association leaders. We also collected relevant documents, such as copies of state content standards. Most of the state-level data collection occurred in the fall of 2003.

District-level data were collected from superintendents through paper-and-pencil surveys in January and February of 2004, 2005, and 2006, and through semistructured telephone interviews in the spring of 2004 and 2006. School-level data were gathered each year through principal and teacher surveys, and annual case studies were conducted in a small subsample of schools. Many of the survey questions appeared in both the principal and teacher surveys, allowing us to compare responses between these groups. Principal and teacher surveys were distributed in January and February of each year, and responses were collected through June. Each survey instrument (superintendent, principal, and teacher) was pilot tested with representatives from the appropriate respondent group using structured "think aloud" cognitive interviews.

Response rates were quite high for each of the three surveys each year. The survey response rate for the superintendent survey was 88 percent in 2003–2004 and 73 percent in 2004–2005 and 2005–2006. The response rate for the principal survey was between 85 and 87 percent each year. The response rate for the teacher survey was 83 percent in 2003–2004, 87 percent in 2004–2005, and 82 percent in 2005–2006 (see Tables A.5, and A.6).

We also conducted annual case study visits to two elementary schools and one middle school in two districts in each state. We interviewed principals, teachers, and other staff, and conducted parent focus groups when principals agreed.

Survey Analyses

To analyze survey responses, we generated state-specific sampling and nonresponse weights for each state. Using these weights, we are able to report statewide estimates of the responses of superintendents, principals, and teachers from regular public schools and districts. Because we excluded some schools that are subject to NCLB requirements but that operate outside a traditional district governance structure, such as charter schools, all of the results generalize only to regular public schools in the respective states. One of the consequences of our sampling strategy in which teachers and principals are nested within schools and schools are nested within districts is that the number of responses grows progressively smaller as we move from teachers to principals to superintendents. As a result, the summary statistics based on teacher responses are more precise than those based on principal responses, which are more precise than those based on superintendent responses. To help the reader interpret the results, we include estimates of the standard errors (SEs) associated with the survey responses in all of the tables in the monograph.

How This Report Is Organized

Chapters Two, Three, and Four present results for California, Georgia, and Pennsylvania, respectively. In each case, we first provide the context in which SBA policies have been implemented and then present results by answering the four research questions listed above. In each of these state-specific chapters, we make comparisons with the other states when the results were significantly different. If one state was different from the other two, we note that in the chapter dedicated to the first state. Many of the findings are similar across the states, and we ask readers to be patient if the results seem familiar; the value of this approach is our ability to describe the findings for each state holistically in the context of that state's local conditions and past experience with accountability. Following the results, we present conclusions in Chapter Five. Information about sampling is contained in Appendix A, and all of the quantitative survey results (including mean responses and SEs) are presented in tabular form in Appendix B.

Technical Notes

A number of different question formats were used in the surveys, and the results are stated in a manner that is consistent with the response options that were given. Most response formats should be familiar to the reader: *strongly agree* to *strongly disagree, no emphasis* to *major emphasis, never* to *often.* Teachers were asked how often they engaged in specific teaching techniques. However, some questions were unique to this survey. For example, a number of questions asked how much a behavior had changed as a result of the introduction of a test or accountability system, and the respondent was given either four options ranging from *not at all* to *a great deal* or three options ranging from *changed for the worse* to *changed for the better.* These questions did *not* designate a specific time period for the change. Other questions asked whether an NCLB-related intervention or activity had occurred, but they did not ask how often the event occurred or how much of the activity had taken place.

Generally, we report in the text only differences that are statistically significant. We do report a handful of differences that are not statistically significant but that we thought were of substantive interest; in these cases, we note explicitly in the text that the differences are not statistically significant. Readers can use the SEs in Appendix B to determine whether other differences are statistically significant or whether they might be the result of measurement or sampling error. As a very rough guideline, the difference between two percentages is statistically significant (at an alpha level of 0.05) if it is larger than twice the sum of the SEs associated with the numbers being compared. In the case of the superintendent survey, in which the number of respondents in each state is small, the SEs are large and only very large differences (sometimes 40 percentage points) will be statistically significant.

To make the monograph easier to read, we report quantitative results in terms of simple fractions (e.g., one-half of teachers, one-third of principals) and we round percentages to the nearest multiple of five. We also use relative language to describe proportions. We use the term *almost all* when greater than 85 percent of respondents answered in a particular way. *Most* is used when between 60 percent and 85 percent of individuals gave the same response. A *majority* means more than 50 percent, and a *minority* means less than 50 percent. *Some* is used when between 15 percent and 40 percent of respondents answered in a certain way, and *few* is used when less than 15 percent of individuals gave a particular response.[4] All of the actual results are presented in Appendix B.

We use the term *educator* to include superintendents, principals, and teachers. The term *administrator* refers to superintendents and principals.

---

[4]   We used similar, but not identical, conventions in our companion monograph. The present monograph covers three years rather than two, and we made the ranges for *almost all, most, some,* and *few* slightly wider because there was greater variation in responses over time.

CHAPTER TWO

Implementation of SBA in California

Background on California's SBA System

California had already developed an SBA system when NCLB was enacted. The California State Board of Education adopted content standards for English language arts and mathematics in 1997 and science, history, and social science in 1998 (California State Board of Education, 2008). These standards cover all grades from kindergarten through twelfth and were deemed to be among the highest-quality state standards in the nation by the Fordham Foundation, whose rankings focus on clarity, rigor, and quality of content (Finn, Petrilli, and Julian, 2006). In 1999, the California legislature passed the Public School Accountability Act (PSAA), which created a test-based accountability system with three main components: a comprehensive testing program, rewards for successful schools, and sanctions for underperforming schools (California Department of Education, 2008).

The testing program combined commercially available norm-referenced tests and custom-developed standards-based tests. Based on test scores, schools were assigned an academic performance index (API). Schools' API scores were based on a weighted combination of scores across subjects. At first, only reading and math scores contributed to the API. Over time, writing, science, history, and social science were added to the formula, although reading and math scores still held the most weight. To avoid sanctions, schools had to increase their APIs each year by 5 percent of the difference between their prior scores and the state interim target. Schools were also required to increase the performance of subgroups of students, although these targets were set somewhat lower because of the larger measurement error associated with smaller groups of students. The API was calculated so that student gains at the bottom of the achievement spectrum led to greater increases in the API than gains at the top of the achievement spectrum.

The PSAA established a number of rewards programs for high-performing schools and their teachers, including the California Staff Performance Incentive Award and the Governor's Performance Award, but these programs were not funded after 2000. The PSAA also established the Immediate Intervention/Underperforming Schools Program (II/USP). Under this program, low-performing schools were offered monetary assistance to develop and implement school improvement plans with the help of an external evaluator approved by the state. If schools failed to show growth in the two implementation years of the improvement plan, they were required to contract with a school assistance and intervention team. In 2001, a new program, the High Priority Schools Grant Program (HPSGP) was established to take the place of II/USP. HPSGP is similar to II/USP but targets money more narrowly to the lowest-performing schools and allows for a longer school-improvement implementation period. HPSGP was still in effect as of the 2005–2006 school year (Harr et al., 2007).

With the passage of NCLB, California had to adapt its existing SBA system to the demands of the new federal law. Perhaps most significantly, California had to subordinate its API growth model for measuring school performance to NCLB's AYP proficiency status model. California decided to use API as the state's additional indicator for elementary and middle schools, so the state did in part retain its growth model approach. However, the hybrid system often sent mixed signals to educators. For example, in 2005 over one-third of all schools were successful according to one measure and not successful according to the other measure (O'Connell, 2006). According to state education officials interviewed in 2004 as part of the ISBA study, many educators preferred the state's system to NCLB. NCLB also accelerated California's shift from norm-referenced tests to standards-based tests, a change that was already starting to occur before NCLB's adoption.

Under NCLB, states design their own assessments and set their own proficiency cutoff scores; studies have shown that the difficulty of these achievement standards varies a great deal across states. California's proficiency cutoff scores have consistently been found to be some of the most challenging among the states (National Center for Education Statistics [NCES], 2007; Cronin et al., 2007). According to NCES, the proficient level on California's fourth grade reading exam maps out to just above the "basic" level on the National Assessment of Educational Progress (NAEP), which places California ahead of 25 of the 32 states in the analysis in terms of rigor and well ahead of Georgia, whose fourth grade reading proficient level corresponds to a NAEP score far below basic (NCES, 2007).[1] The proficient level on California's eighth grade reading exam maps to a NAEP score between basic and proficient, as does the proficient level on its fourth grade mathematics exam; in each case, California's exams ranked higher in rigor than those of most of the other states in the study (NCES, 2007). The Fordham Foundation conducted a similar analysis, mapping state exams to the Northwest Evaluation Association's Measures of Academic Progress (MAP) and found similar results for California (Cronin et al., 2007). The Fordham Foundation mapped proficiency cutoff scores on state reading and math exams in grades three through eight to the MAP, and in each case, California ranked fourth or higher of the 26 states studied. California, like the other states in our study, set its AMO starting

---

[1]   Pennsylvania was not one of the states in that analysis.

point based on schoolwide average proficiency levels from the 2001–2002 school year (see Hamilton et al., 2007, footnote 5). As a result, in the 2002–2003 school year, 13.6 percent of students in each subgroup were required to be proficient in English language arts (ELA), and 16 percent were required to be proficient in mathematics. These starting points were markedly lower than in the other states we studied (see Figures 2.1 and 2.2). This difference is due in part to differences in the student populations in the three states and also to the rigor of California's standards. Because California's AMO starting point was low, the state's AMO trajectory is necessarily quite steep, requiring schools to substantially increase the percentage of students reaching proficiency from 2004 to 2005 (the middle year of our study), and from 2007 to 2014.

Perhaps partly because of its rigorous standards, California has had higher percentages of its schools fail to make AYP, be identified for improvement, and be placed in corrective action than the two other states we studied (see Table 2.1). California also has a more diverse student population than the other states, so its schools are more likely to have significant subgroups for NCLB purposes. Schools with greater numbers of subgroups are less likely to make AYP because they must meet a greater number of targets.

Figure 2.1
Annual Measurable Objectives for Reading and ELA, Grades Three Through Eight, by State, 2002–2014

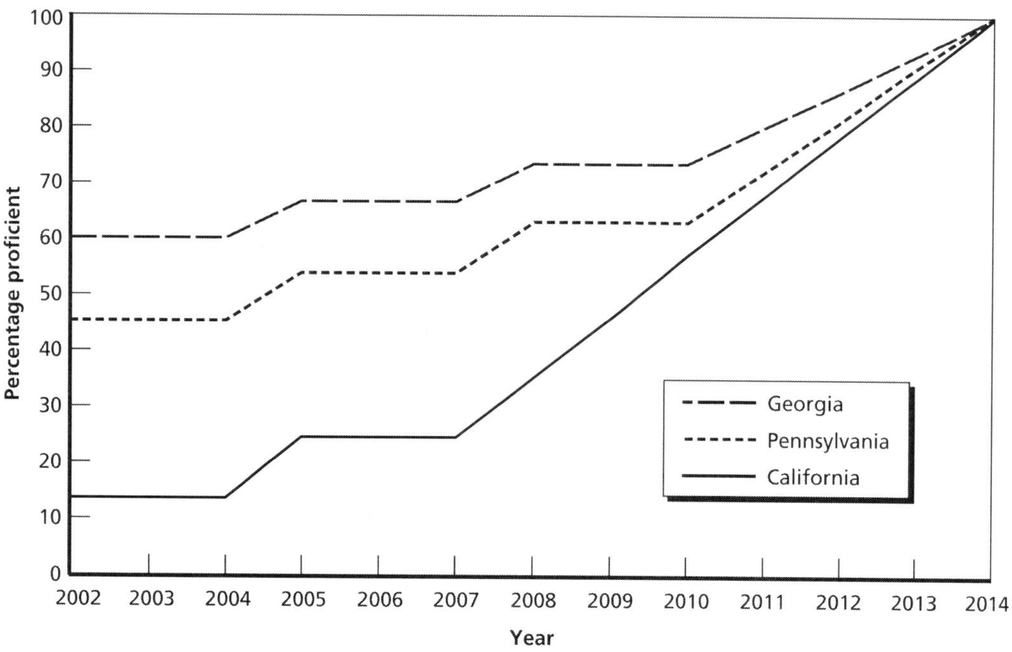

Figure 2.2
Annual Measurable Objectives for Mathematics, Grades Three Through Eight, by State, 2002–2014

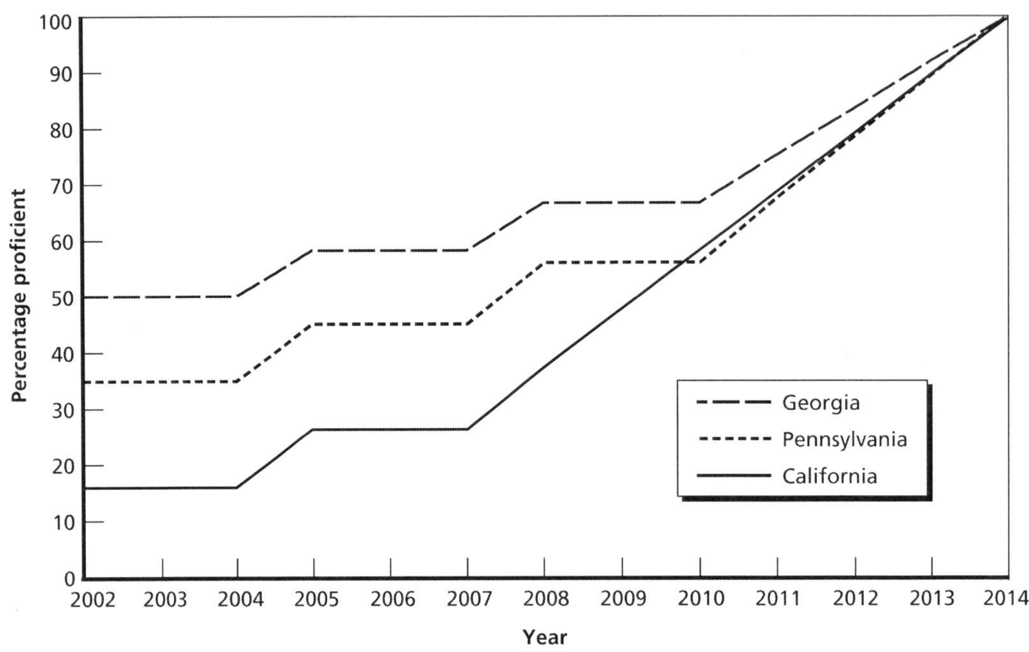

California Findings from the ISBA Study

How Did Districts, Schools, and Teachers Respond to State Accountability Efforts, Including State Standards and State Tests?

California mathematics and science content standards were perceived to be useful, but local curriculum was not always aligned with standards. Each year, over 80 percent of the mathematics and science teachers in California reported that the state standards were useful for planning their lessons. However, over three-quarters of mathematics teachers and about two-thirds of science teachers reported that the state standards include more content than could be adequately covered in a school year. At the same time, a growing minority of elementary school teachers (about 15 percent in 2004 and about one-quarter in 2006), about one-quarter of middle school math teachers, and about 40 percent of middle school science teachers reported that the standards omitted important topics that were part of their curriculum. Figure 2.3 shows that despite finding the standards useful, many teachers had concerns about the alignment of standards with their curriculum. Thus, in teachers' judgments, the standards

Table 2.1
NCLB Status

School Status	California (%)		Georgia (%)		Pennsylvania (%)	
	2004–2005[a]	2005–2006[b]	2004–2005[a]	2005–2006[b]	2004–2005[a]	2005–2006[b]
Made AYP	65	62	82	79	77	79
Identified for improvement	13	10	12	10	5	5
Corrective action	2	4	1	2	1	3
Restructuring	3	4	4	3[c]	2	3

SOURCE: Data were retrieved from the state departments of education Web sites on April 17, 2007.

NOTE: Schools must make AYP for two consecutive years to exit from improvement status, so some schools may be counted in both the "made AYP" and "identified for improvement" rows. The percentages in the last three rows are mutually exclusive.

[a] Based on 2003–2004 testing.

[b] Based on 2004–2005 testing.

[c] Years four through nine of school improvement.

may embody unrealistic expectations for how much content can be covered, and there remains some misalignment between the content of the mathematics and science standards and the content of their curriculum (see Tables B.1 and B.2).

School and district administrators were more likely than teachers to perceive mathematics and science assessments as good measures of student achievement. In 2006, about two-thirds of superintendents (down from 95 percent in 2004) and over 60 percent of principals thought that state assessments accurately reflected student achievement. However, in each year fewer than one-half of mathematics teachers reported that the assessments were a good measure of students' mastery of state content standards. Figure 2.4 shows that principals were generally more likely than teachers to see state assessments as valid indicators of student achievement. Many mathematics and science teachers were also concerned with the difficulty of state assessments and their alignment with curriculum. Each year, about one-half of mathematics teachers reported that the mathematics assessments were too difficult for the majority of their students, about one-third of mathematics teachers reported that assessments included content not in their curriculum, and about one-third reported that assessments omitted content that was in their curriculum. (Teachers' opinions about state assessments are consistent with their opinions about state standards reported above.) Higher percentages of science teachers agreed that science assessments were too difficult for a majority of students and included content not in their curriculum (see Tables B.3 to B.5).

Figure 2.3
California Teachers Agreeing with Statements About State Content Standards, 2006

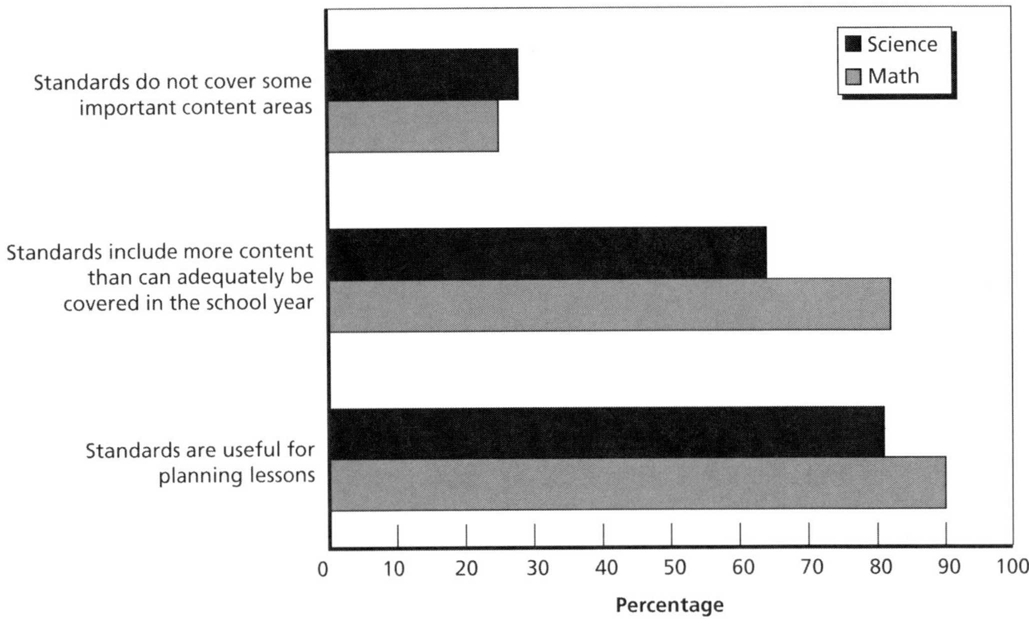

Test results were widely available and were widely used by district administrators, principals, and teachers. Each year, almost all principals reported that test results for the school as a whole, for student subgroups, and for content subtopics were available to them. Similarly, about 90 percent of mathematics teachers reported that test results were available to them by subgroup and by subtopic in 2006, representing a slight increase from 2004 among elementary school teachers. However, fewer than half of principals and only about two-thirds of teachers reported receiving results in a timely manner in each year (see Tables B.6 to B.10).

Each year, almost all superintendents reported that assessment results were helpful for district and school planning, focusing PD, and curriculum reform. Across all three years, large majorities of principals said they found the state test results useful for planning school improvement and curriculum reform, and for identifying students who need extra support (over 80 percent in each case). Also in each year, over 70 percent of elementary school principals and over two-thirds of middle school principals found state test results to be useful for focusing PD. One-third to two-thirds of principals reported that the data were useful for making decisions regarding student promotion and retention and for identifying teachers' strengths and weaknesses (see Tables B.11 and B.12).

Figure 2.4
California Educators Agreeing That State Assessment Scores Accurately Reflect Student Achievement (Principals) or Are Good Measures of Student Mastery (Teachers)

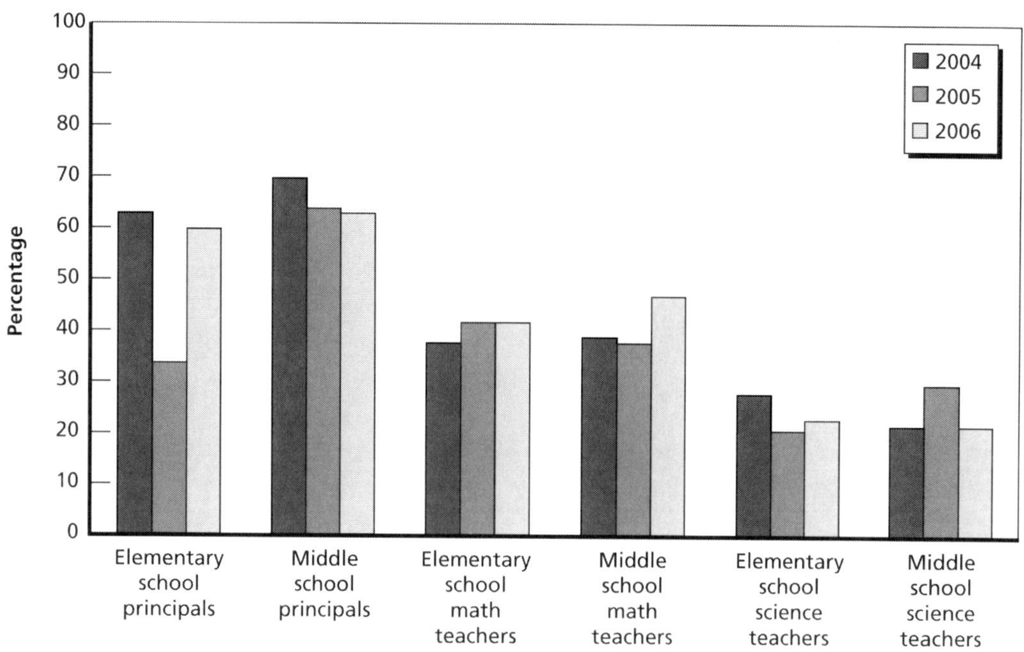

RAND *MG784-2.4*

Across the three years, most mathematics teachers, about half of elementary school science teachers, and one-half or fewer of middle school science teachers said the state test results were useful for identifying gaps in curriculum and instruction and identifying areas in which they needed to strengthen their content knowledge. About one-half of mathematics teachers (and a lower percentage of science teachers) reported that the test results were useful for tailoring instruction to individual student needs. Generally, middle school teachers found test results to be less useful in tailoring instruction than did elementary school teachers. About one-third of the mathematics teachers who had access to subgroup results said they were useful to them, and about two-thirds of math teachers who had access to subtopic results said they were useful to them as well. Each year, one-third to two-thirds fewer science teachers than math teachers reported that subgroup and subtopic results were useful to them (see Tables B.13, B.8, and B.9).

Superintendents increasingly promoted the use of periodic progress tests[2] in addition to the annual state test, and teachers found the progress tests to be helpful for improving teaching and learning. In 2005 and 2006, roughly one-half of superintendents reported

---

[2]   Progress tests are formal assessments given periodically during the year to measure student progress in mastering state standards. They are also called interim tests, formative tests, and benchmark tests. To our knowledge, these exams do not result in any consequences for teachers in the districts we studied.

that their district required schools to adopt periodic progress testing to monitor student learning in mathematics.[3] The percentage of math teachers who reported that they were required to administer progress tests increased from 2004 to 2006, although the change was not statistically significant for elementary school teachers. According to teachers, the progress test requirements were much more common in mathematics than in science and more common in elementary school mathematics than in middle school mathematics. Typically progress tests were administered two to three times per year. A growing majority of teachers in schools that used progress tests reported that the progress test was a good measure of student mastery (from about one-half in 2004 to about two-thirds in 2006), and about three-quarters said the progress test helped them identify and correct gaps in curriculum and instruction (see Tables B.14 to B.18). Figure 2.5 shows that each year a majority of teachers found both annual state tests and progress tests useful for identifying and correcting gaps in curriculum and instruction; however, larger proportions of teachers found the progress tests, as opposed to the state tests, useful for this purpose.

California educators reported that they understood the state accountability system, but not all agreed that AYP status was a good reflection of their students' performance or that AYP targets would be attained in future years. Eighty percent or more of California administrators reported that they understood the AYP criteria used in the state and that they received help to understand all the accountability system requirements. On the other hand, about one-half of teachers reported that the system was too complicated to understand. Each year, one-half or more of school principals agreed that their school's AYP status reflected the overall performance of their students, and 40 to 60 percent of superintendents thought the district's AYP status correctly reflected the performance of students. Principals in schools that made AYP were more likely to agree that AYP was an accurate reflection of student performance than principals in schools that did not. In 2006, more than three-quarters of principals and superintendents thought their school or district would make AYP the next year, but far fewer (half of elementary school principals, one-third of middle school principals and fewer than one-quarter of district superintendents) believed they would continue to make AYP over the next five years. Opinions about whether their schools and districts would make AYP did not change much over the three years (see Tables B.19 to B.23).

What School Improvement Strategies Were Used, and Which Were Perceived to Be Most Useful?

School improvement efforts incorporated a wide repertoire of strategies. Each year, almost all principals reported using four strategies to improve school performance, including matching curriculum and instruction with standards and/or assessments, using existing research, providing additional instruction to low-performing students, and

---

[3] We did not ask this question in 2004.

Figure 2.5
California Teachers Agreeing That Annual State Tests and Progress Tests Are Helpful in Identifying and Correcting Gaps in Curriculum and Instruction

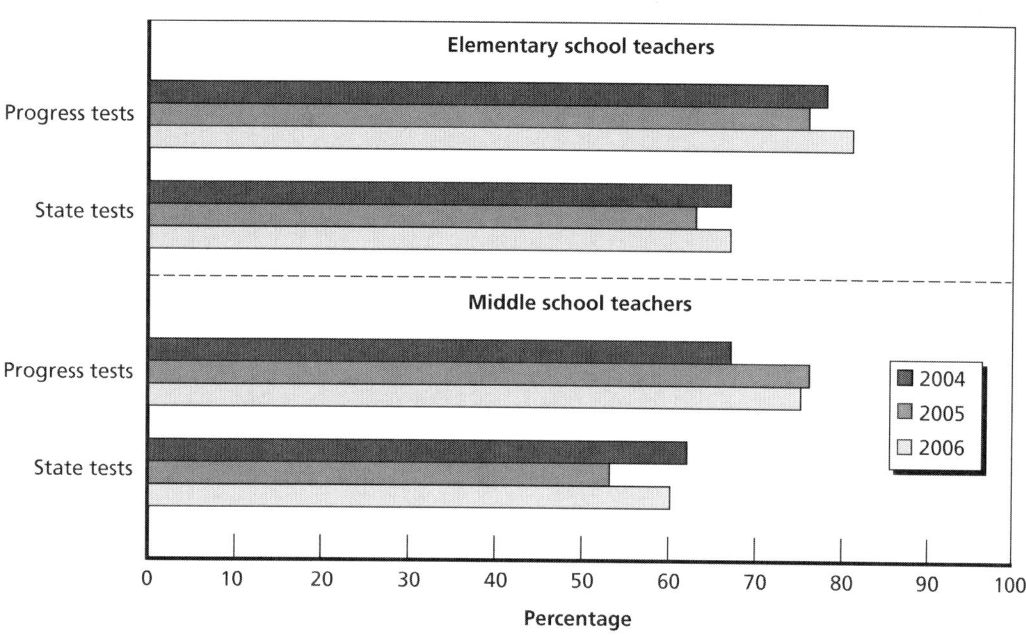

increasing the use of data. Over three-quarters of principals reported using three additional strategies, which included increasing teacher PD, improving the school planning process, and providing programs outside of regular school hours. Efforts to make the school more attractive to parents and to restructure the school day were less prevalent but still common, with more than half of principals reporting that they employed these strategies. Less than one-third of principals reported increasing instructional time by lengthening the school day or year or shortening recess (see Table B.24).

Focusing on low-performing students, alignment, and data use were the most important school improvement strategies according to principals. For the most part, principals reported focusing on the same school improvement strategies each year. The following strategies were reported as most important in 2005 by the largest proportions of principals: providing additional instruction to low-performing students (about 40 percent of elementary school principals and about 55 percent of middle school principals), matching curriculum and instruction with standards and/or assessments (just over half of all principals), and increasing the use of achievement data to inform instruction (about 70 percent of elementary school principals and about 40 percent of middle school principals). Principal reports of the most important improvement strategies were quite similar in 2006 (see Table B.25).

California principals reported that their schools and districts engaged in a wide variety of test preparation activities. Over 85 percent of principals reported that their schools and/or districts were engaged in one or more forms of test preparation. The most commonly reported practices were identifying content that is likely to appear on the state test (90 percent or more each year) and discussing methods for preparing students to take tests (over 80 percent each year). Smaller majorities of principals reported that they distributed released copies of the state test or test items and encouraged teachers to focus on students near the proficient level (bubble kids). About half of principals also distributed commercial test preparation materials (e.g., practice tests), and half encouraged or required teachers to spend more time on tested subjects and less on other subjects. The reported distribution of released copies of the state test or test items increased from 2004 to 2006 (from about 40 percent to over half), but it was still lower than in the other states we studied, as was the use of commercial test preparation materials. There are a couple of possible explanations for this difference. First, California's accountability system has been in place longer than Georgia's and Pennsylvania's, so educators and students may have been more familiar with the state tests in California. Second, California regulations and guidelines published by the California Department of Education required educators to limit the use of test preparation activities in order to ensure test validity (California Department of Education, 2004). We found evidence through our case studies that educators were getting the message; one principal told us, "We hear horror stories of 'you'd better not use that practice test because this is too identical to the CST [California Standards Test], and we'll get dinged'" (see Table B.26).

According to superintendents, districts provided a range of support to principals and teachers for school improvement. In 2005 and 2006, two-thirds or more of superintendents reported that their district implemented each of the following strategies to help schools align curriculum and instruction with standards in mathematics: providing sample lessons linked to state standards, monitoring implementation of state standards in classrooms, and mapping out the alignment of required textbooks and instructional programs to state standards.[4] These strategies were less commonly used for science; in each case, about one-half of the districts reported engaging in the strategy. Each of these district actions was reported to be useful in aligning math curriculum and instruction to standards by one-half to three-quarters of teachers (in general, slightly fewer than in the other two states we studied) (see Tables B.27 to B.30).

Each year, a majority of principals reported that their districts provided necessary assistance to schools when they were having difficulties, appropriate support to enable principals to act as instructional leaders, and appropriate instructional support for teachers. Each year, three-quarters or more of superintendents reported that their districts helped some or all schools obtain additional PD to apply the results of "sci-

---

[4]   These questions were not asked in 2004.

entifically based research" about education; more than 20 percent of superintendents reported assigning additional full-time school-level staff to support teacher development in some or all schools; and between 15 and 40 percent provided a coach or mentor to assist the principal in some or all schools. In addition to PD, three-quarters or more of districts provided technical assistance to some or all schools in each of a number of other areas, including analyzing assessment data, school improvement planning, preparing complete and accurate data to comply with NCLB reporting requirements, implementing effective instructional strategies, and helping to teach grade-level standards to English language learners (ELLs) and student with disabilities (this last question was not asked in 2004). This technical assistance was typically offered to all schools, not just those that were low performing (see Tables B.31 and B.32).

Superintendents also reported that districts intervened and required schools to take certain actions to improve student performance. For example, in 2006 about three-quarters of districts required some or all elementary and middle schools to offer remedial assistance to students outside the normal school day[5] (an increase in the case of middle schools from just under half in 2004). Similarly, a growing percentage of districts (from fewer than half in 2005 to more than half in 2006) required elementary schools and middle schools to increase the amount of instruction that low-achieving students received in mathematics, but few required increased time for low-achieving students in science (less than 15 percent each year for middle schools and less than 10 percent each year for elementary schools). In addition, a substantial but decreasing percentage of districts required schools, particularly middle schools, to implement new mathematics or science curricula; from 2004 to 2006, the percentage of districts requiring middle schools to implement new curricula declined from more than 60 percent to about 30 percent in mathematics and from more than 30 percent to around 15 percent in science. This decline makes sense. Early on in our study, districts may have been responding to the new demands of NCLB by adopting new curricula that were more rigorous and/or better aligned to state standards. We would not expect districts that recently adopted new curricula to revise them again within one or two years (see Tables B.33 to B.35).

Only 17 schools were identified for improvement in our sample, so our estimates for these schools are much less precise than our estimates for all schools. However, in these schools the most common forms of district or state assistance were additional PD resources, special grants to support school improvement, and a mentor or coach for the principal (e.g., a distinguished educator). There were only a handful of schools in corrective action in our sample (see Tables B.36 and B.37).

PD emphasized the alignment of curriculum and instruction with standards as well as other improvement strategies. Each year, about two-thirds of teachers reported that a major emphasis of the PD they received was on aligning curriculum and instruc-

---

[5]   Other than the NCLB-required supplemental educational services.

tion with standards. In addition, each of the following topics received strong emphasis according to about half of teachers: instructional strategies for low-achieving students, instructional strategies for ELLs, and mathematics and mathematics teaching. The emphasis on ELLs was greater in California than in the other states we studied. About one-third of teachers said that PD had a major focus on interpreting and using student test results, although this was more common among elementary school teachers than among middle school teachers in 2005 and 2006 (see Table B.38).

According to superintendents, the California Department of Education often, but not always, provided needed technical assistance to their districts. In 2005 and 2006, almost all districts that reported needing assistance clarifying accountability system rules and requirements reported receiving it.[6] In each of the two years, over three-quarters of districts that reported needing help developing and implementing district improvement plans received this assistance from the state, and over half of districts received needed assistance in the following areas: identifying effective methods and instructional strategies in scientifically based research, providing effective PD, and using data more effectively. Districts were more likely to report unmet needs in other areas. Only one-third to one-half of districts that needed assistance developing curricular materials based on content standards received it. Only about 40 percent of districts that reported needing help promoting parent involvement received assistance from the state in this area in each year (see Table B.39).

What Was the Impact of Accountability on Curriculum, Teacher Practice, and Student Learning?

Educators' reports about the effects of accountability on curriculum and instruction grew more positive from 2004 to 2006, but substantial proportions of educators still believed that the accountability system was having a negative effect on morale. The proportion of elementary school principals who agreed that the academic rigor of the curriculum had changed for the better grew from about 40 percent to about 80 percent from 2004 to 2006. During the same period, the proportion of teachers agreeing with this statement grew from about one-third to about one-half. The proportion of middle school principals agreeing that the academic rigor of the curriculum had improved held steady from 2004 to 2006 at 50 percent. Figure 2.6 shows an increase from 2004 to 2006 in the percentage of elementary school principals, elementary school teachers, and middle school teachers who reported that academic rigor of the curriculum had improved. Fewer than 20 percent of principals or teachers reported that academic rigor had changed for the worse, and these percentages declined or remained about the same from 2004 to 2006. Similar results were found regarding schools' focus on student learning. For example, the proportion of elementary school principals reporting an improved focus on student learning as a result of accountability increased from

---

[6]   We did not ask this question in 2004.

Figure 2.6
California Educators Agreeing That the Academic Rigor of the Curriculum Had Improved as a Result of Accountability

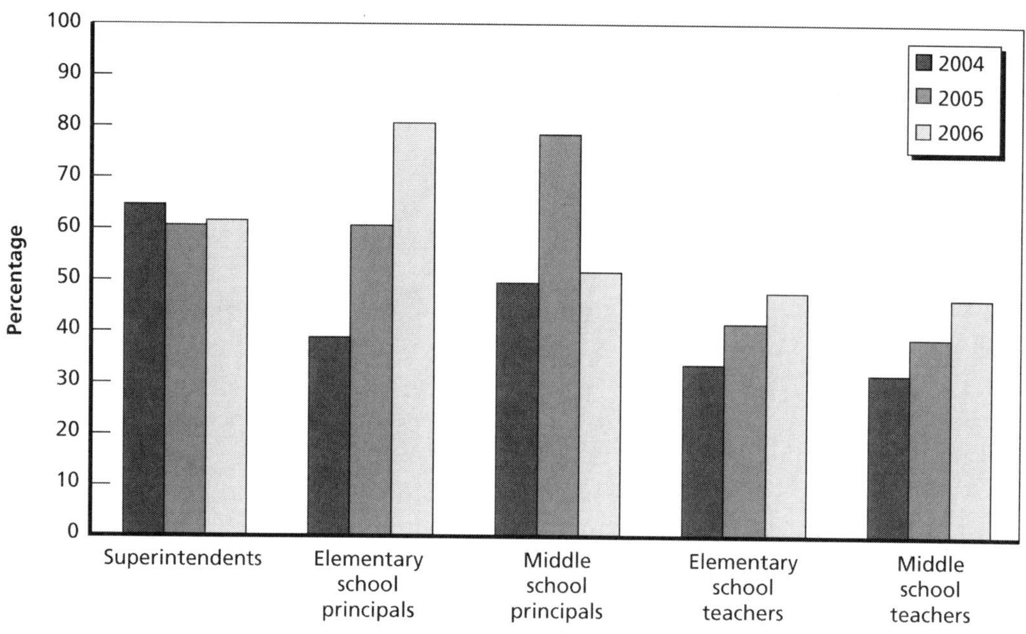

less than 60 percent in 2004 to over 80 percent in 2006. A growing majority of elementary school principals (from just over half to about 80 percent) and 70 percent or more of middle school principals reported that the accountability system was beneficial for students, but only about one-third of teachers agreed (see Tables B.40 and B.41).

By 2006, about half of teachers reported that their teaching practices had improved as a result of the accountability system (an increase from about one-third in 2004). A growing minority of teachers said their relations with their students had improved, as well (from less than 15 percent in 2004 to about one-quarter in 2006 for elementary school teachers and from 10 percent to about 20 percent for middle school teachers). A shrinking majority of mathematics teachers (from about three-quarters in 2004 to just over half in 2006) and 30 to 40 percent of science teachers reported that the state tests caused them to search for more-effective teaching methods. In 2006, about two-thirds of middle school mathematics teachers and about half of middle school science teachers said the state tests caused them to offer more assistance outside of the school day to students who are not proficient, compared with about one-quarter of elementary school mathematics teachers and 10 percent of elementary school science teachers (responses were similar in 2004 and 2005) (see Tables B.42 to B.44).

In 2006, most superintendents and middle school principals reported that coordination of the mathematics curricula across grades had changed for the better as a result of accountability. In the case of middle school principals, this represented a significant increase from 2004; there was some variation across years in the case of superintendents but no easily discernible pattern. Forty to 50 percent of elementary school principals concurred with this assessment each year. Across all three years, about one-quarter of elementary school principals and fewer than half of middle school principals reported improvements in the coordination of the science curriculum across grades as a result of accountability, while the remainder reported no change. The responses from superintendents on the coordination of the science curriculum fluctuated from year to year; about 20 percent reported that coordination improved in 2004 compared with just over one-half in 2005, and less 15 percent in 2006 (see Table B.45).

Finally, about three-quarters of superintendents, just under one-half of teachers and elementary school principals, and one in five middle school principals reported that staff morale had changed for the worse as a result of the accountability system in 2006 (see Figure 2.7). Fewer principals and teachers reported a negative effect on morale in 2006 than in 2004, and this decrease was especially marked in the case of principals (see Table B.46).

Teachers responded to standards-based accountability by aligning their curriculum with standards but did not report changing specific teaching techniques. Teachers reported making a lot of changes in curriculum and instruction in response to standards-based accountability. Perhaps the most widespread change involved aligning curriculum and instruction with standards and, to a lesser extent, with assessments. In each year, almost all math teachers and over three-quarters of science teachers reported that they had aligned their instruction with the standards; more than half of all teachers also reported aligning instruction with the state assessments (see Table B.47).

The state tests were an explicit factor in teachers' reported changes in practice. Each year, over two-thirds of elementary school math teachers and just under half of elementary school science teachers reported that they focused more on standards *as a result of the state test.* About two-thirds of elementary school math teachers and about one-quarter of elementary school science teachers also reported focusing more on topics emphasized on the assessment because of the state test. Somewhat smaller proportions of middle school teachers reported focusing more on standards and topics emphasized on the assessment as a result of the state test (see Tables B.43 and B.44).

It appears that teachers' efforts to improve alignment did not typically involve changing the amount of time devoted to specific subjects, at least during the time period we studied. In each year, one-half to two-thirds of teachers reported no changes in the amount of time students spent in each of the following subjects: mathematics, reading/language arts, science, social studies, arts/music, and physical education. In 2006, about 20 percent of elementary school teachers reported increases in the time they spent on mathematics (a slight decline from 2004), and about 30 percent reported increases in time for reading/language arts. Smaller proportions of middle school teachers reported increases in time in math and reading. There were few reports of decreases

Figure 2.7
California Educators Agreeing That Staff Morale Had Changed for the Worse as a Result of Accountability

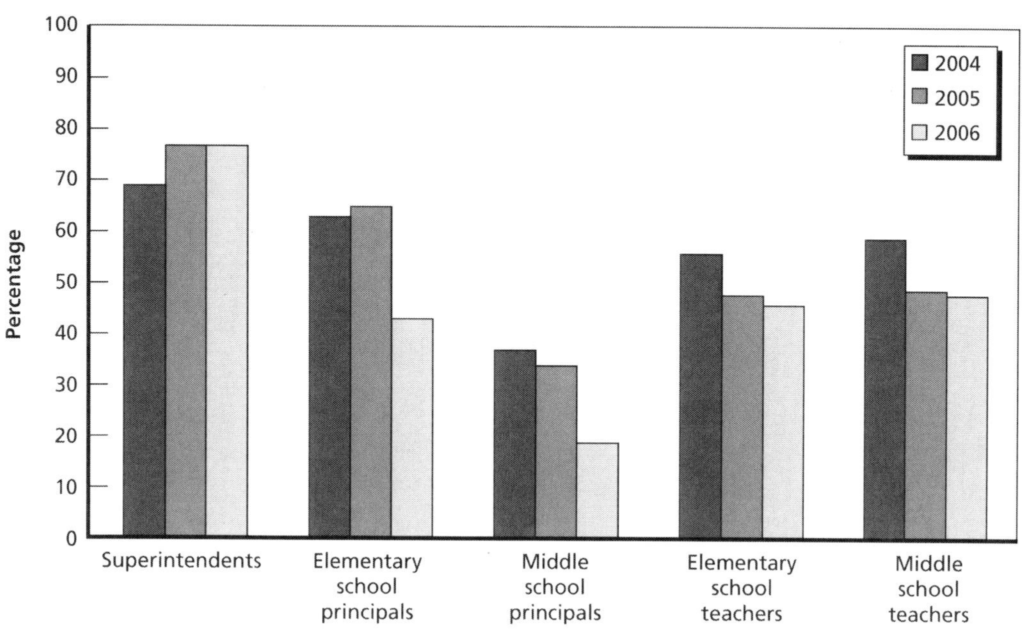

RAND *MG784-2.7*

in time on these two subjects. However, some elementary school teachers indicated that they decreased the amount of time they spent on arts/music, social studies, or science (between 15 and 28 percent for each subject in each year). It is important to note that we asked teachers about changes over the past year in the amount of time allocated to subjects. As a result, teachers' responses would not be expected to reflect cumulative changes since the enactment of NCLB.[7] Thus, it is possible that these findings underestimate the amount of time reallocated between subjects as a result of NCLB's accountability provisions (see Tables B.48 and B.49).

In general, elementary and middle school mathematics and science teachers' reports about particular teaching techniques were similar and did not change much from 2005 to 2006.[8] Almost all mathematics teachers reported that they sometimes or often used most of the techniques mentioned in the survey,[9] including introducing content through formal presentations or direct instruction, assigning homework, reviewing assessments, reteaching topics because performance did not meet expec-

---

[7] In addition, we did not track individual teacher responses over time, so we cannot combine reported annual changes across the three years to estimate cumulative change.

[8] We did not ask this question in 2004.

[9] *Sometimes* was defined as once or twice per month; *often* was defined as once a week or more.

tations, and having students help other students learn content. Over half of science teachers reported using the techniques listed above. In contrast, only about 45 percent of elementary school mathematics teachers and one-third of middle school mathematics teachers reported having students work on extended mathematics investigations or projects in each year. In both 2005 and 2006, about 70 percent of elementary school science teachers and about 80 percent of middle school science teachers reported having students do hands-on laboratory science activities or investigations (see Tables B.50 to B.53).

About half of teachers were concerned that the focus on test scores deprived high-achieving students of challenging curriculum. About one-half of teachers reported in 2005 and 2006 that high-achieving students were not receiving an appropriately challenging curriculum as a result of the accountability system.[10] Other survey responses offer possible explanations for this concern. Each year, over 80 percent of teachers felt that the accountability system left little time to teach material that is not on the state test. This can be viewed as a positive outcome given that SBA is designed to ensure that students master the content outlined in state standards and measured by the assessments. However, this narrow focus on the standards may exclude teaching advanced material that could benefit high-achieving students. We also found evidence that some teachers were giving special attention to certain groups of students. In 2006, over one-third of math teachers (representing a slight increase among elementary school math teachers) and over 10 percent of science teachers said the state tests caused them to focus more on students near the proficient level (bubble kids) than they would have absent the tests (perhaps at the expense of students farther to the extremes of the achievement spectrum) (see Tables B.54, B.43, and B.44).

What Conditions Hindered Improvement Efforts?

Inadequate funding, inadequate materials, and insufficient time were the factors most often reported to hinder efforts to improve performance. Resources are always a concern in education, and each year more than 80 percent of superintendents and more than 60 percent of principals reported that lack of adequate funding was a moderate to great hindrance to their improvement efforts. In contrast, each year fewer than one-third of superintendents or principals reported that inadequate facilities interfered with improvement efforts. In 2006, about 15 percent of superintendents said shortages of standards-based curriculum materials were a problem, down from about one-third in 2004. Each year, one-quarter to one-third of teachers reported that inadequate instructional materials hindered students' academic success (see Tables B.55 and B.56).

Shortages of time to perform administrative functions, prepare for lessons, and deliver instruction were also reported to hinder improvement efforts. In 2005 and 2006, about two-thirds of principals reported that their administrative staff had insuf-

---

[10] We did not ask this question in 2004.

ficient time to perform their duties.[11] Each year, over one-half of middle school teachers and over 70 percent of elementary school teachers reported that there was insufficient class time to cover the curriculum. In addition, in 2005 and 2006 over half of elementary school teachers and about 40 percent of middle school teachers reported that there was inadequate planning time built into the school day. Responses from principals were similar; about 40 percent of middle school principals and more than one-half of elementary school principals reported that lack of teacher planning time was a hindrance to school improvement in both 2005 and 2006[12] (see Tables B.57 to B.59).

Teachers reported that large class sizes and a wide range of student abilities in class were hindrances to student academic success. Each year, about three-quarters of teachers reported that the wide range of student abilities they had to address in class was a hindrance to students' academic success. Similarly, about two-thirds of middle school teachers and over half of elementary school teachers reported that large class sizes hindered students' academic success (see Tables B.60 and B.56).

Most superintendents reported that districts had adequate capacity to support school improvement. Across all three years, majorities of superintendents reported that their districts had adequate staff capacity to provide schools support in most areas we studied. These areas included facilitating improvement in low-performing schools, helping schools analyze data for school improvement, and aligning curriculum with standards. More than half of superintendents reported that they had adequate capacity to provide PD for principals and teachers in 2004 and 2006 (for some unknown reason, capacity to conduct PD dipped in 2005) (see Table B.61).

Many superintendents and principals reported that improvement efforts were hindered by shortages of key staff and shortages of high-quality PD. In 2006, three-quarters of superintendents reported that shortages of mathematics teachers hindered improvement efforts, and 60 percent of superintendents reported that shortages of science teachers were a hindrance, reflecting marked increases from 2005.[13] In addition, each year about 40 percent of superintendents reported that their improvement efforts were hindered by shortages of high-quality PD opportunities for principals or teachers, and principals responded similarly. About one-quarter of principals reported a lack of highly qualified teachers in 2006, and a similar percentage reported shortages of qualified aides or paraprofessionals (responses were similar across the three years) (see Table B.57).

Most teachers reported that students' lack of basic skills and lack of parental support impeded their efforts to improve student achievement. Across the three years, 75 to 80 percent of teachers reported that their efforts to improve student achievement were hindered by students' inadequate basic skills or prior preparation. Similar percentages of teachers reported that they were hindered in their efforts to improve student per-

---

[11] We did not ask this question in 2004.

[12] We did not ask this question in 2004.

[13] We did not ask this question in 2004.

formance by lack of support from parents. For example, the responses from California teachers in 2006 are displayed in Figure 2.8. Student absenteeism and tardiness were concerns for slightly smaller proportions of teachers (see Table B.60).

Most administrators reported that changes in state policies and state leadership, as well as compliance with teacher association policies, were impediments to improvement. Each year, more than two-thirds of superintendents said frequent changes in state policy or leadership were hindrances to improvement. On the other hand, few superintendents reported that disagreements with their school boards over policies hindered their improvement efforts, although this was an issue in one-quarter to one-third of districts in the other states we studied. Each year, more than one-half of superintendents reported that complying with teacher association rules or policies hindered their improvement efforts. About 10 percent of middle school principals and one-third of elementary school principals said frequent changes in district policy or district leadership hindered their improvement efforts in 2006 (see Table B.62).

Some principals reported that a lack of guidance for teaching special-needs populations was a hindrance to their school improvement efforts. In 2005 and 2006, over one-third of elementary school principals and over one-quarter of middle school principals reported that a lack of guidance for teaching standards for special education students (i.e., students

Figure 2.8
California Teachers Reporting That Selected Conditions Were Moderate or Great Hindrances to Students' Academic Success

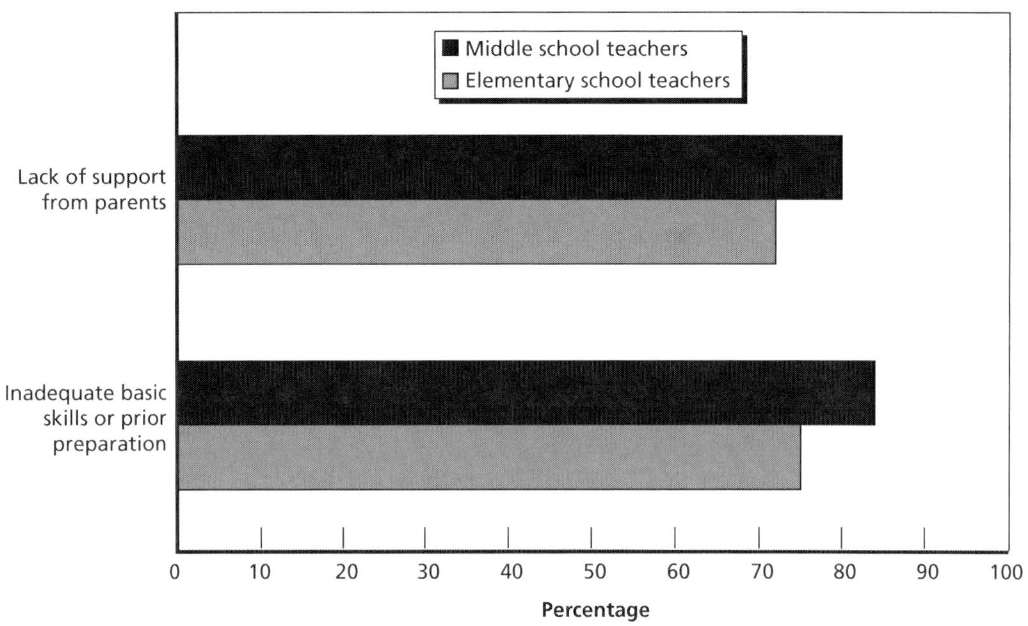

in individualized education programs [IEPs]) was a moderate or great hindrance to their school improvement efforts. About half of elementary school principals and a growing minority of middle school principals (from about 15 percent in 2005 to about 45 percent in 2006) cited the same concern in reference to ELLs. Elementary school principals in California were more likely to report that a lack of guidance for teaching ELLs hindered their school improvement efforts than were elementary school principals in Georgia and Pennsylvania (see Table B.63). This is consistent with the fact that California has a higher percentage of ELLs than do the other two states.

CHAPTER THREE

Implementation of SBA in Georgia

Background on Georgia's SBA System

Georgia was in the process of creating an SBA system in 2001 when NCLB was enacted. Georgia has had academic standards in some form for over 20 years. The state Quality Basic Education Act of 1985 created the Quality Core Curriculum (QCC), which covered reading, ELA, mathematics, science, social studies, foreign languages, fine arts, health, physical education, technology and career education, and agriculture. The standards described what students should learn in each grade from kindergarten to eight and in high school focusing primarily on facts to be learned rather than broader concepts. However, an external audit by Phi Delta Kappa in 2002 found the QCC to be of poor quality, citing lack of depth, focus, and alignment to national standards (Georgia Department of Education, undated).[1] In response to the audit, Georgia launched an initiative in 2002 to develop new standards. In 2003, the state board of education began adopting the Georgia Performance Standards (GPS), a more concept-focused document. The Fordham Foundation gave the new standards high marks, citing their clarity, detail, and organization (Finn, Petrilli, and Julian, 2006).

Georgia also had a comprehensive testing program prior to NCLB, which included tests in reading, mathematics, and science in grades one to eight. These tests were revised following the adoption of GPS to align with the new standards. In 2000, the Georgia State A Plus Education Reform Act created a test-based accountability system patterned on those in Texas and North Carolina. Under this system, schools were to be awarded a letter grade (A–F), which would determine whether the school received rewards or was subjected to sanctions. NCLB was enacted just as A Plus was being implemented, and subsequently the system was altered to conform to the federal policy.

---

[1] In a 2004 review of the Georgia performance standards, Phi Delta Kappa evaluated the standards' validity by comparing them with national standards published by the International Reading Association, the National Council for Teachers of English, the National Council of Teachers of Mathematics, the National Council for the Social Studies, and the National Committee on Science Education Standards and Assessment (see Poston et al., 2004).

In 2005, Georgia introduced the state single accountability system (SSAS), which integrated A Plus with NCLB, and this remains the current SBA system in Georgia. Under SSAS, AYP is the dominant measure of school performance. SSAS also includes rewards for schools with the highest percentage of students meeting or exceeding standards on the state assessments and for Title I schools that make AYP for three or more consecutive years. Sanctions for consistently underperforming schools include school-level interventions (e.g., appointing instructional coaches, replacing staff, and making governance changes) and district-level interventions (e.g., appointment of a school district support specialist). If schools continue to underperform, they can be compelled to enter into an improvement contract with their school district, which includes oversight by the Georgia Department of Education.

Georgia's achievement standards have been found to be less rigorous than those of California. According to an analysis by NCES, which mapped state proficiency standards onto NAEP, Georgia's achievement standards for fourth and eighth grade reading and mathematics are among the lowest of the 36 states studied (NCES, 2007). The proficient level on the Georgia fourth grade mathematics assessment is equivalent to the low end of the "basic" range on NAEP, and the proficient level on the eighth grade mathematics assessment and the fourth and eighth grade reading assessments corresponds to "below-basic" NAEP scores. Like the other states in our study, Georgia based its AMO starting point on schoolwide average proficiency scores from 2001–2002. In 2002–2003, 50 percent of students were expected to demonstrate proficiency in mathematics and 60 percent were expected to demonstrate proficiency in reading and ELA. These starting points were substantially higher than those in California and Pennsylvania, perhaps reflecting the lesser difficulty of Georgia's academic standards (see Figures 2.1 and 2.2). Because Georgia has less ground to make up than California and Pennsylvania in reaching 100 percent proficiency, its AMO trajectory is less steep. In addition, the required gains are most heavily concentrated from 2010 to 2014. As with the other two states in our study, Georgia's AMO target increased in the middle year of our data collection, 2004–2005, but not in the other two years in which we collected data.

In 2005–2006, 79 percent of Georgia schools were identified as having made AYP based on the previous year's test scores, a significantly higher percentage than in California and roughly equal to the percentage in Pennsylvania. Nevertheless, Georgia had a higher percentage of its schools in improvement status, corrective action, or restructuring than did Pennsylvania (see Table 2.1).

Georgia Findings from the ISBA Study

How Did Districts, Schools, and Teachers Respond to State Accountability Efforts, Including State Standards and State Tests?

Georgia mathematics and science standards were perceived to be useful, but local curriculum was not always aligned with standards. Each year, over 80 percent of mathematics and science teachers in Georgia reported that the state standards were useful for planning their lessons. However, in 2006 about one-half of mathematics teachers and science teachers reported that the state standards include more content than could be adequately covered in a school year. The percentages of math and science teachers who reported that the standards included too much content declined by almost 20 points during the three years of the study, and they were lower than the percentages in the other states we studied. In all three years and in both subjects (mathematics and science), more middle school teachers than elementary school teachers reported that the standards contained more content than could reasonably be covered in a year. This response was given despite the fact that the new GPS for mathematics were implemented in the sixth grade in 2004–2005 and in the seventh grade in 2005–2006. New GPS for science were implemented in middle schools in 2004–2005 and in grades three through five the next year. At the same time, over 20 percent of mathematics teachers and about one-third of science teachers reported each year that the standards omitted important topics that were part of their curriculum. Figure 3.1 shows that despite finding the standards useful, many teachers had concerns about the alignment of standards with their curriculum. Thus, in teachers' judgments, the standards may embody unrealistic expectations for how much content can be covered, and there remains some misalignment between the content of the mathematics and science standards and the content of the curriculum (see Tables B.1 and B.2).

School and district administrators were more likely than teachers to perceive mathematics and science assessments as good measures of student achievement. Consistently across the three years, over two-thirds of superintendents and about two-thirds of principals thought that state assessments accurately reflected student achievement. However, in each year only slightly more than half of mathematics teachers and slightly fewer than half of science teachers reported that the assessments were a good measure of students' mastery of standards. Figure 3.2 shows that principals were more likely than teachers to see state assessments as valid indicators of student achievement. Given that substantial proportions of teachers did not believe that state assessments were good measures of students' content mastery, it is not surprising that sizable minorities of teachers reported concerns about these assessments. One-fourth to one-third of mathematics teachers reported that the mathematics assessments were too difficult for the majority of their students, included content not in their curriculum, or omitted content that was

Figure 3.1
Georgia Teachers Agreeing with Statements About State Content Standards, 2006

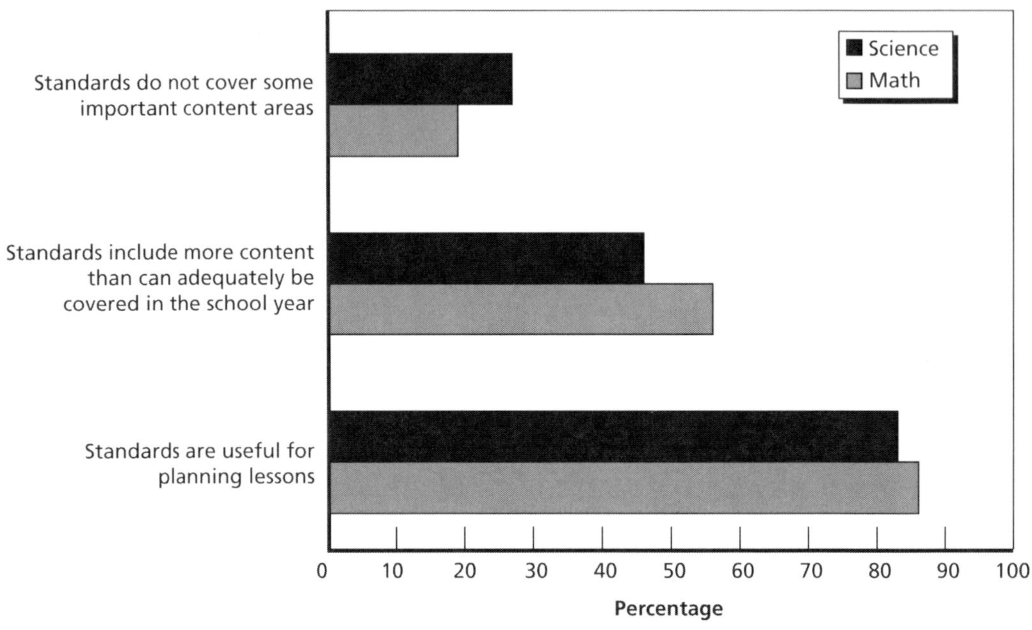

in their curriculum. Slightly higher percentages of science teachers found fault with the science assessments on the same grounds. However, in general, Georgia educators were more favorable toward the quality of state assessments than were educators in the other states we studied (see Tables B.3 to B.5).

Test results were widely available and were widely used by district administrators, principals, and teachers. Test results were available in a variety of formats, and they appeared to be available in a much more timely manner in 2006 than 2004. Each year, almost all principals reported that test results for the school as a whole, for student subgroups, and for subtopics were available to them. Similarly, over 85 percent of mathematics teachers and three-quarters of science teachers reported that test results were available to them by subgroup and by subtopic in 2006 (an increase from 2004). By 2006, over one-half of principals and three-quarters of teachers reported receiving results in a timely manner (an increase from fewer than one-quarter of principals and fewer than half of teachers in 2004) (see Tables B.6 to B.10).

Each year, almost all superintendents reported that assessment results were helpful for district and school planning, focusing PD, and curriculum reform. Three-quarters or more of principals said they found the state test results useful for each of the following activities: planning school improvement, PD, curriculum reform, and identifying students who need extra support. Increasing majorities of principals also reported that

Figure 3.2
Georgia Educators Agreeing That States Assessment Scores Accurately Reflect Student Achievement (Principals) or Are Good Measures of Student Mastery (Teachers)

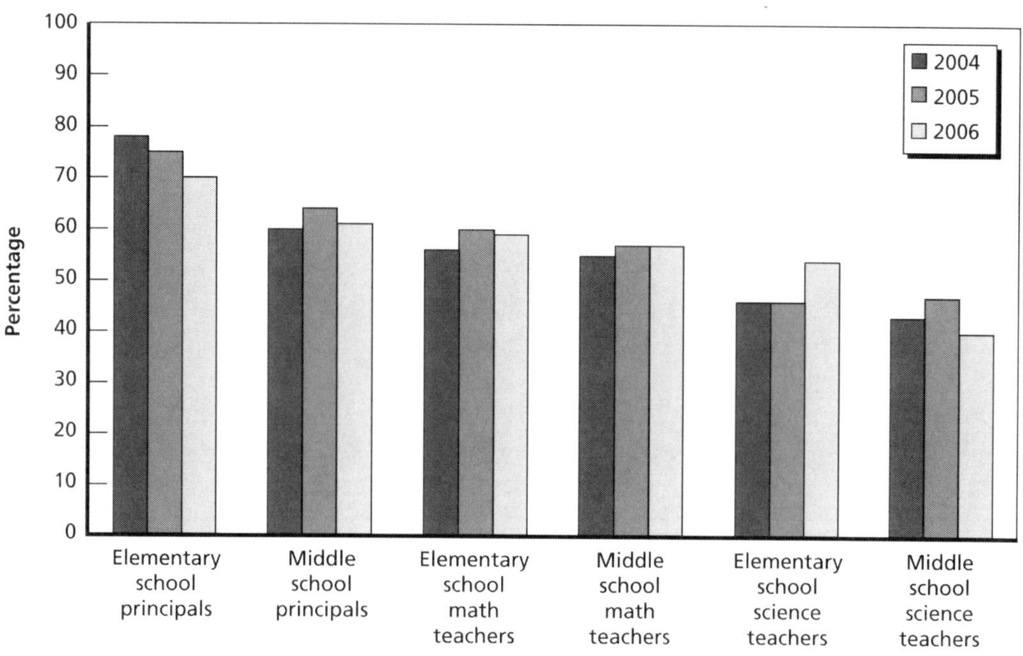

RAND MG784-3.2

the data were useful for making decisions regarding student promotion and reten-tion (from about 70 percent in 2004 to about 90 percent in 2006) and for identifying teachers' strengths and weaknesses (from about two-thirds in 2004 to about three-quarters in 2006) (see Tables B.11 and B.12).

Each year, over two-thirds of teachers said the state test results were useful for identifying gaps in curriculum and instruction, identifying areas in which they needed to strengthen their content knowledge, and tailoring instruction to individual student needs (higher percentages than in the other states we studied). In 2005 and 2006, just over half of the mathematics teachers who had access to subgroup results said they were useful to them, and over three-quarters who had access to subtopic results said they were useful to them, as well (both sets of responses increased from 2004) (see Tables B.13, B.8, and B.9).

Superintendents promoted the use of periodic progress tests[2] in addition to the annual state test, and teachers found the progress tests to be helpful for improving teaching and learning. In 2005 and 2006, over 70 percent of superintendents reported that their

---

[2] Progress tests are formal assessment given periodically during the year to measure student progress in master-ing state standards. They are also called interim tests, formative tests, and benchmark tests. To our knowledge, these exams do not result in any consequences for teachers in the districts we studied.

district required schools to administer periodic progress tests to monitor student learning in mathematics, and 40 to 65 percent required progress tests in science (considerably higher than in the other states we studied).[3] The percentage of math teachers who reported that they were required to administer progress tests increased from 2004 to 2006 (although the difference was not statistically significant in the case of middle school teachers). According to teachers, the progress test requirements were most common for elementary school math, followed by middle school math, middle school science, and finally elementary school science. Most frequently, progress tests were administered every six to eight weeks, although many teachers also reported progress tests being administered only two to three times per year. Each year, over 60 percent of teachers in schools that used progress tests reported that the progress test was a good measure of student mastery (a slightly higher percentage than for the annual state tests) and that the progress tests helped them identify and correct gaps in curriculum and instruction. Figure 3.3 shows that each year most elementary school teachers and middle school teachers found annual state tests and progress tests useful for identifying and correcting gaps in curriculum and instruction. The use of progress testing was

Figure 3.3
Georgia Teachers Agreeing That Annual State Tests and Progress Tests Are Helpful in Identifying and Correcting Gaps in Curriculum and Instruction

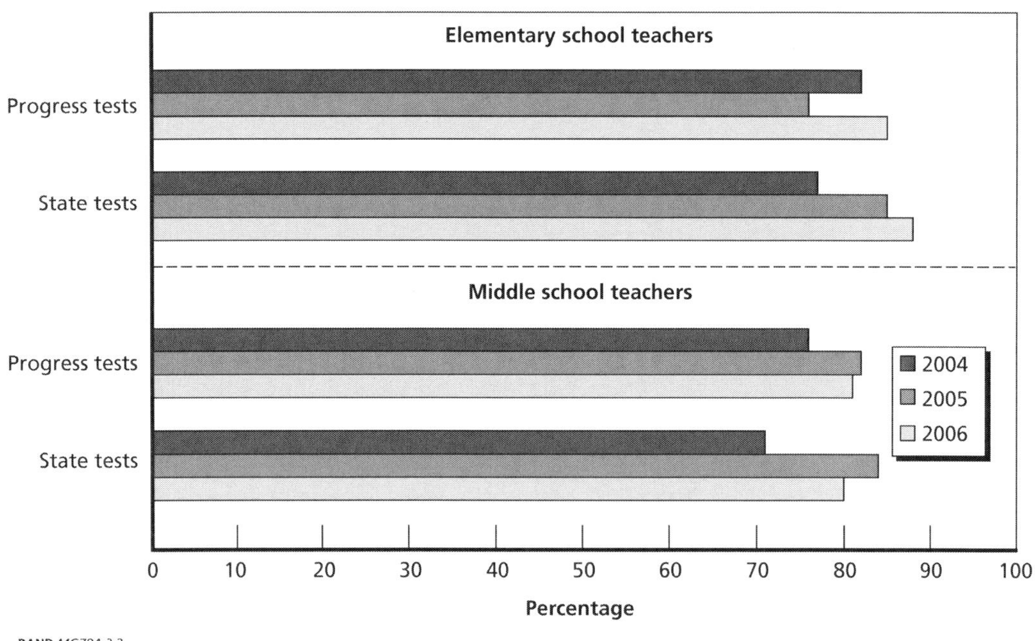

---

[3] We did not ask this question in 2004.

more common in Georgia than in the other states we studied, especially for science (see Tables B.14 to B.18).

Georgia educators reported that they understood the state accountability system, but not all agreed that AYP status was a good reflection of their students' performance or that AYP targets would be attained in future years. Each year, nearly all Georgia administrators reported that they understood the AYP criteria being used in the state and that they received help to understand all the accountability system requirements. However, a declining proportion of elementary school teachers (from one-half in 2004 to just over one-third in 2006) and over 40 percent of middle school teachers reported that the system was too complicated to understand. By 2006, over 80 percent of elementary school principals agreed that their school's AYP status reflected the overall performance of their students (up from about two-thirds in 2004), but slightly fewer than half of middle school principals and superintendents concurred. Principals in schools that made AYP were more likely to agree that AYP was an accurate reflection of student performance than principals in schools that did not. In 2006, almost all principals and superintendents thought their schools or districts would make AYP the next year (an increase from 2004 for both superintendents and middle school principals), and a somewhat smaller majority of principals and superintendents believed they would continue to make AYP over the next five years (see Tables B.19 to B.23).

What School Improvement Strategies Were Used and Which Were Perceived to Be Most Useful?

School improvement efforts incorporated a wide repertoire of strategies. Each year, almost all principals reported using seven strategies to improve school performance, including matching curriculum and instruction with standards and/or assessments, using existing research, providing additional instruction to low-performing students, increasing the use of data, increasing teacher PD, improving the school planning process, and providing programs outside of regular school hours. Less prevalent, but still commonly reported by principals, were efforts to make the school more attractive to parents (two-thirds to three-quarters of principals each year), to restructure the school day (over one-half of principals each year), and to lengthen the school day or school year (one-third to one-half of principals) (see Table B.24).

Alignment, data use, and focusing on low-performing students were the most important school improvement strategies according to principals. In both 2005 and 2006, the strategies reported as most important by the largest proportions of principals were matching curriculum and instruction with standards and/or assessments (over half of all principals each year), increasing the use of achievement data to inform instruction (60 percent or more of principals each year), and providing additional instruction to low-performing students (just under half of principals each year) (see Table B.25).

Georgia principals reported that their schools and districts engaged in a wide variety of test preparation activities. Each year, almost all principals reported that their schools and/or districts were engaged in one or more forms of test preparation, including identifying content that is likely to appear on the state test, discussing methods for preparing students to take tests, distributing released copies of the test or test items, and encouraging teachers to focus on students near the proficient level (bubble kids) (see Table B.26).

According to superintendents, districts provided a range of support to principals and teachers for school improvement. In 2005 and 2006, 60 percent or more of superintendents reported that their districts implemented each of the following strategies to help schools align curriculum and instruction with standards in mathematics and science: providing feedback on the implementation of standards in classrooms, aligning textbooks and instructional programs with standards and assessments, developing "pacing plans" or "instructional calendars," establishing detailed curriculum guidelines, and providing sample lessons.[4] Teachers typically found these district support strategies to be useful in aligning math curricula and instruction with standards (see Tables B.27 to B.30).

Each year, more than three-quarters of principals reported that their district provided needed assistance to schools when they were having difficulties, appropriate support to enable principals to act as instructional leaders, and appropriate instructional support for teachers. Each year, almost all superintendents reported that their districts helped some or all schools obtain additional PD based on scientifically based research, and more than half provided a coach or mentor to assist the principal in some or all schools. More than two-thirds of superintendents reported assigning additional full-time school-level staff to support teacher development in some or all schools in 2006, up from about 40 percent in 2004. Georgia superintendents were more likely to report providing staff to support teacher development and coaches for principals than were superintendents in the other states we studied. In addition to PD, almost all districts provided technical assistance to schools in a number of other areas, including analyzing assessment data, school improvement planning, implementing effective instructional strategies, and helping to teach grade-level standards to ELLs and to student with disabilities. This technical assistance was generally offered to all schools, not just those that were low performing (see Tables B.31 and B.32).

Superintendents also reported that districts intervened and required schools to take certain actions to improve student performance. For example, in 2006 over 80 percent of districts required some or all elementary schools to offer remedial assistance to students outside the normal school day, and three-quarters required the same of middle schools (2005 responses were similar). Similarly, in 2005 and 2006, about 90 percent of districts required middle schools to increase the amount of instruction that low-achieving students received in mathematics and about one-third required increased time for low-achieving students in science. The proportion

---

[4]   We did not ask this question in 2004.

of districts that required elementary schools to increase the amount of mathematics instruction for low-achieving students decreased dramatically from almost all in 2005 to just half in 2006, while the proportion of districts requiring elementary schools to increase science instruction remained steady at about one-third. In addition, a small but growing percentage of districts required middle schools to implement new mathematics or science curricula. From 2004 to 2006, the percentage of districts requiring middle schools to implement new curricula grew from fewer than 20 percent to more than 40 percent in mathematics and from fewer than 10 percent to more than 30 percent in science. About one-third of districts required elementary schools to implement new math curricula each year, and a smaller proportion required elementary schools to implement new science curricula (see Tables B.33 to B.35).

There were only 21 schools identified for improvement in our 2006 sample, so our estimates for identified schools are not as precise as our estimates for all schools. However, in these schools the most common forms of district or state assistance were additional PD resources, special grants to support school improvement, a mentor or coach for the principal (e.g., a distinguished educator), or a school support team. There were only five schools in corrective action in our 2006 sample (see Tables B.36 and B.37).

PD emphasized the alignment of curriculum and instruction with standards as well as other improvement strategies. In 2004, two-thirds of teachers reported that a major emphasis of the PD they received was on aligning curriculum and instruction with standards, and this percentage rose to over three-quarters by 2006. One-half or more of teachers each year reported that the following topics received strong emphasis: instructional strategies for low-achieving students, preparing students to take state assessments, and mathematics and mathematics teaching. Slightly more than half of teachers said that PD had a major focus on interpreting and using student test results in 2006, a slight increase from 2004 (see Table B.38).

Districts reported that the state met their current needs for technical assistance. In 2005 and 2006, 70 to 80 percent of districts reported that they needed technical assistance for each of the following purposes: identifying effective instructional methods and strategies, providing effective PD, and using data more effectively.[5] Almost all superintendents reported that they received the technical assistance they needed in these areas in 2005 and 2006. Similarly, most to all districts reported that they received the technical assistance they needed in most other areas (e.g., clarifying accountability system rules and requirements, developing and implementing a district improvement plan, and working with schools in need of improvement). Districts were less likely to receive technical assistance in promoting parent involvement; just over half of superintendents who needed assistance in this area received it in each year. Districts in Georgia were generally more likely than districts in the other two states to report receiving sufficient technical assistance from the state (see Table B.39).

---

[5] We did not ask this question in 2004.

What Was the Impact of Accountability on Curriculum, Teacher Practice, and Student Learning?

Educators' reports about the effects of accountability on curriculum and instruction grew more positive from 2004 to 2006, although a minority of teachers continued to believe that the accountability system was having a negative effect on morale. The proportion of principals who agreed that the academic rigor of the curriculum had changed for the better grew from just over one-half to about three-quarters from 2004 to 2006. During the same period, the proportion of teachers agreeing with this statement grew from about 40 percent to about half. Figure 3.4 shows the percentage of educators who reported that the academic rigor of the curriculum improved. (The increases were not statistically significant in the case of superintendents and elementary school principals). Few principals or teachers reported that academic rigor had changed for the worse. Positive results were found regarding the school's focus on student learning, as well. Growing majorities of principals (from about 70 percent in 2004 to about 85 percent in 2006) and teachers (from about half in 2004 to about 60 percent in 2006) reported an improved focus on student learning as a result of accountability. There were also small increases during this period in the proportion of educators reporting that the accountability

Figure 3.4
Georgia Educators Agreeing That the Academic Rigor of the Curriculum Had Improved as a Result of Accountability

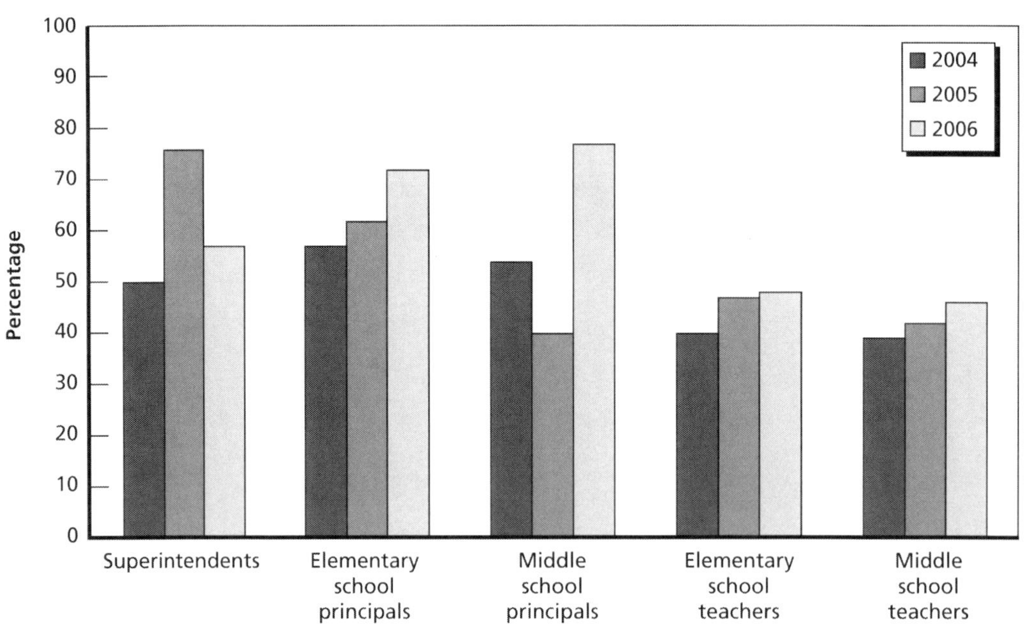

system was beneficial for students (from slightly fewer than half to slightly more than half among teachers and from about two-thirds to over three-quarters among principals) (see Tables B.40 and B.41).

Each year, slightly more than half of teachers reported that their teaching practices had improved as a result of the accountability system, and over one-quarter said their relations with their students had improved, as well. Over two-thirds of teachers reported that, as a result of the state test, they searched for more-effective teaching methods. Each year, 70 to 80 percent of middle school teachers said they offered more assistance outside of the school day to students who were not proficient as a result of the test-based accountability system, compared with 15 percent of elementary science teachers and about one-third of elementary mathematics teachers (see Tables B.42 to B.44).

In 2006, the majority of superintendents and principals reported that coordination of the mathematics and science curricula across grades had changed for the better as a result of accountability, representing a marked increase from 2004 among superintendents. In contrast, about half of teachers reported in 2004 that staff morale had changed for the worse as a result of the accountability system; that percentage had declined to about 40 percent by 2006 (see Figure 3.5 and Tables B.45 and B.46).

Figure 3.5
Georgia Educators Agreeing That Staff Morale Had Changed for the Worse as a Result of Accountability

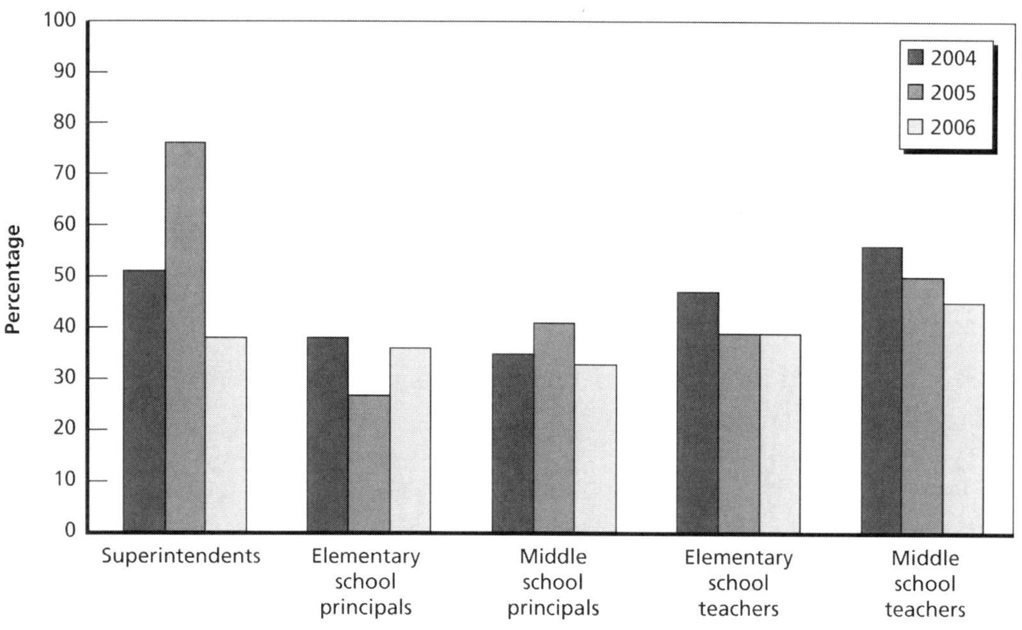

Teachers responded to standards-based accountability by aligning their curriculum with standards and assessments but did not report changing specific teaching techniques. Teachers reported making a lot of changes in curriculum and instruction in response to SBA. Perhaps the most widespread change involved aligning curriculum and instruction with standards and assessments. Each year, over 80 percent of teachers reported that they had aligned their instruction with the standards, and about 80 percent also reported aligning instruction with the state assessments (see Table B.47).

The state tests were an explicit factor in teachers' reported changes in practice. Each year, most elementary school teachers reported that the state assessments caused them to focus more on standards, focus more on topics emphasized in the assessment, and place more emphasis on question styles and formats from the test. Middle school teachers were less likely to report that the state assessment caused them to focus more on assessment topics (just under half each year) and place more emphasis on assessment question styles and formats (just over half each year) (see Tables B.43 and B.44).

It appears that teachers' efforts to improve alignment did not typically involve changing the amount of time devoted to specific subjects, at least during the time period we studied. Each year, over 60 percent of elementary school teachers and about half of middle school teachers reported no change in the amount of time students were exposed to each subject (math, science, reading/language arts, social studies, arts/music, and physical education). Only about 20 percent of teachers reported increases in the time spent on mathematics or reading/language arts, and there were few reports of decreases in time on these two subjects. However, small but consistent minorities of teachers, particularly elementary school teachers (usually between 10 and 15 percent), indicated that they decreased the amount of time they spent on arts/music, social studies, or science. We asked teachers about changes during the past year in the amount of time allocated to subjects.[6] As a result, we cannot estimate cumulative changes since the enactment of NCLB. It is possible that these findings underestimate the cumulative amount of time reallocated among subjects as a result of NCLB's accountability provisions (see Tables B.48 and B.49).

In general, elementary and middle school mathematics and science teachers' reports about particular teaching techniques were similar and did not change much from 2005 to 2006. Almost all mathematics and science teachers reported that they sometimes or often used most of the techniques included in our survey, including introducing content through formal presentations or direct instruction, assigning homework, and having students help other students learn content. In contrast, only about one-half of elementary school mathematics teachers and one-third of middle school mathematics teachers reported having students work on extended mathematics investigations or

---

[6]   In addition, we did not track individual teacher responses over time, so we cannot combine reported annual changes across the three years to estimate cumulative change.

projects, but over 80 percent of science teachers reported having students do hands-on laboratory science activities or investigations (see Tables B.50 to B.53).

About half of teachers were concerned that the focus on test scores deprived high-achieving students of challenging curriculum. About one-half of teachers reported in 2005 and 2006 that high-achieving students were not receiving an appropriately challenging curriculum as a result of the accountability system.[7] Other survey responses offer possible explanations for this concern. Each year, over 80 percent of teachers felt that the accountability system left little time to teach material that is not on the state test. This can be viewed as a positive outcome given that SBA is designed to ensure that students master the content outlined in state standards and measured by the assessments. However, this narrow focus on the standards may exclude teaching advanced material that could benefit high-achieving students. We also found evidence that some teachers were giving special attention to certain groups of students. Substantial minorities of teachers (typically between 30 and 40 percent) said the state tests caused them to focus more on students near the proficient level (bubble kids) than they would have absent the test (perhaps at the expense of students farther to the extremes of the achievement spectrum), and there were small increases in these percentages between 2004 and 2006 among elementary school teachers (Tables B.54, B.43, and B.44).

What Conditions Hindered Improvement Efforts?

Inadequate funding, inadequate materials, and insufficient time were reported to hinder efforts to improve performance. Resources are always a concern in education, and each year over 80 percent of superintendents reported that lack of adequate funding was a moderate to great hindrance to their improvement efforts. A declining proportion of principals concurred; by 2006, only about 45 percent of elementary school principals and about 60 percent of middle schools principals reported that inadequate funding was a hindrance (each was down from about three-quarters in 2004). The proportion of administrators reporting that inadequate facilities interfered with improvement efforts also declined, from over 20 percent to about 10 percent of principals and from 30 percent to only about 5 percent of superintendents. About 40 percent of superintendents said shortages of standards-based curriculum materials were a problem in 2006, similar to previous years. Superintendents' judgments were confirmed by teachers; each year, approximately one-third of teachers reported that inadequate instructional materials hindered students' academic success (see Tables B.55 and B.56).

Shortages of time for planning, administration, and instruction were also reported to hinder improvement efforts. In 2006, about two-thirds of principals reported that they had insufficient staff time to perform their administrative duties, an increase from about half in 2005.[8] Each year, about one-half of teachers reported that there was

---

[7]   We did not ask this question in 2004.

[8]   We did not ask this question in 2004.

insufficient class time to cover the curriculum, and about 40 percent reported that there was inadequate planning time built into the school day. In both cases, elementary school teachers were more likely to be concerned about time than were middle school teachers. Responses from principals were similar; in 2005 and 2006, about 20 percent of middle school principals and about 40 percent of elementary school principals reported that lack of teacher planning time was a hindrance to school improvement[9] (see Tables B.57 to B.59).

Teachers reported that large class sizes and a wide range of student abilities in class were hindrances to student academic success. Each year, about two-thirds of teachers reported that the wide range of student abilities they had to address in class was a hindrance to students' academic success. Similarly, each year slightly more than one-half of middle school teachers and slightly less than one-half of elementary school teachers reported that large class sizes hindered students' academic success (see Tables B.60 and B.56).

Most superintendents reported that districts had adequate capacity to support school improvement. Each year, two-thirds or more of superintendents reported that their districts had adequate staff capacity to provide schools support in most areas we studied, including facilitating improvement in low-performing schools and helping schools analyze data for school improvement. The proportion of superintendents reporting that they had adequate capacity to conduct PD for teachers and principals increased from about one-third in 2004 to about two-thirds in 2006 (see Table B.61).

A minority of districts and schools were hindered by shortages of highly qualified principals, highly qualified mathematics and science teachers, and high-quality PD opportunities for principals and teachers. Each year, over one-quarter of superintendents reported a lack of qualified principals. According to superintendents, shortages of qualified mathematics and science teachers hindered efforts to improve performance in about two-thirds to three-quarters of districts each year. Across the three years, a substantial minority of superintendents (between 15 percent and 45 percent) reported that their improvement efforts were also hindered by shortages of high-quality PD opportunities for principals or teachers; principals cited this concern in smaller proportions. Shortages of qualified aides or paraprofessionals were a less frequently reported problem (fewer than 20 percent of principals identified this as a hindrance each year) (see Table B.57).

Most teachers reported that students' lack of basic skills and lack of parental support impeded their efforts to improve student achievement. Each year, about 70 percent of elementary school teachers and over 80 percent of middle school teachers reported that their efforts to improve student achievement were hindered by students' inadequate basic skills or prior preparation. Similar percentages of teachers reported that they were hindered in their efforts to improve student performance by lack of support from parents. In 2006, most elementary school and middle school teachers reported that inade-

---

[9]   We did not ask this question in 2004.

quate basic skills or prior preparation and lack of support from parents were hindrances to students' academic success (see Figure 3.6). Student absenteeism and tardiness were concerns for one-half of elementary school teachers and two-thirds to three-quarters of middle school teachers (see Table B.60).

Administrators reported that changes in state policies and state leadership were impediments to improvement in many districts and schools. Each year, most superintendents said frequent changes in state policy or leadership were hindrances to improvement. In 2006, one-third of superintendents reported that disagreements with their school boards over policies hindered their improvement efforts, more than twice the proportion in 2004. However, in contrast to the other states we studied, but as we would expect in a state with few teacher unions, few Georgia superintendents reported that complying with teacher association rules or policies hindered their improvement efforts. Each year, fewer than 20 percent of principals said frequent changes in district policy or district leadership hindered their improvement efforts (see Table B.62).

Some principals reported that a lack of guidance for teaching special-needs populations was a hindrance to their school improvement efforts. In 2005 and 2006, 15 to 30 percent of elementary school principals and 20 to 40 percent of middle school principals reported that a lack of guidance for teaching standards to special

Figure 3.6
Georgia Teachers Reporting That Selected Conditions Were Moderate or Great Hindrances to Students' Academic Success

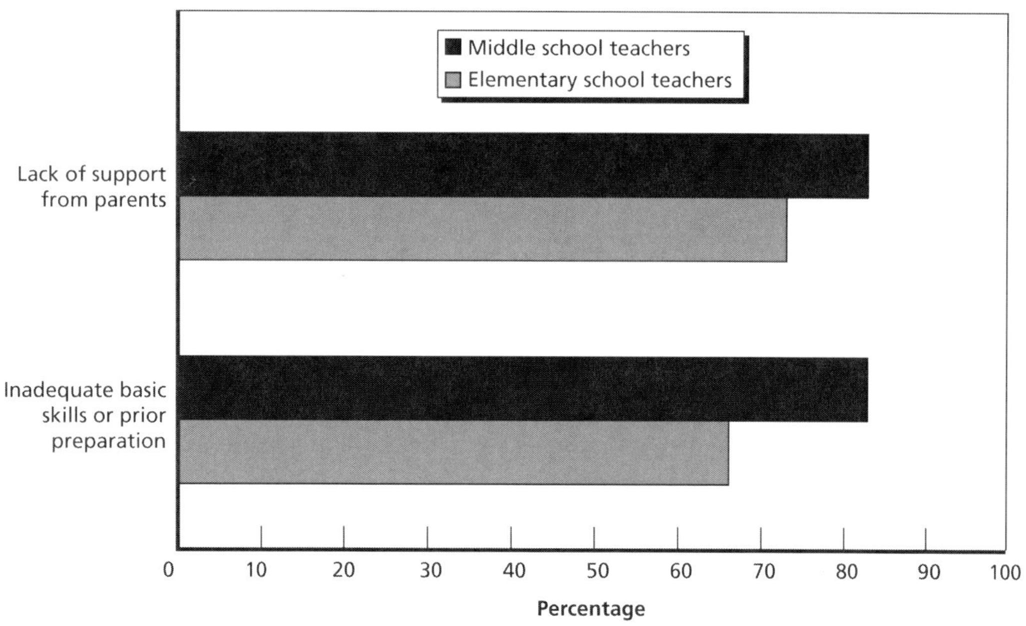

education students was a moderate or great hindrance to their school improvement efforts. About 20 percent of elementary school principals and between 20 and 30 percent of middle school principals reported the same concern in reference to ELLs (see Table B.63).

CHAPTER FOUR

Implementation of SBA in Pennsylvania

Background on Pennsylvania's SBA System

Of the three states in the ISBA study, Pennsylvania had the least developed SBA system prior to NCLB. Pennsylvania has a tradition of local control in education, with minimal interference from the state. Prior to NCLB, Pennsylvania had content standards and testing for reading and math in grades three, five, eight, and eleven, and science standards in grades four, seven, ten, and twelve. The Pennsylvania State Board of Education academic standards were cumulative, describing what students should know by the end of the grade, including material learned in earlier grades. However, the standards were not designed to indicate what material would be assessed on the Pennsylvania System of School Assessment (PSSA). Despite its tradition of local control, the state was starting to play a somewhat larger role in education prior to NCLB. For example, in 2000, the Pennsylvania General Assembly passed the Education Empowerment Act (Article XVII-B), which allowed the state to identify low-performing districts as *education empowerment districts*. Once districts were labeled as empowerment districts, the state gave local boards of education expanded powers to improve schools by reopening them as charters schools, reconstituting them, or restructuring them in other major ways.

NCLB forced Pennsylvania to make a number of changes to its education system. The content standards were revised to include new "assessment anchors," which describe what material is assessed at each grade level. Starting in 2006, students were tested in math and reading in all grades from three to eight as well as in grade eleven; in the 2007–2008 school year, science testing was added for grades four, eight, and eleven. In 2004, Pennsylvania created the Pennsylvania Performance Index (PPI), which is a continuous improvement measure that is based on improvements at all levels of the PSSA. Pennsylvania allowed schools to appeal their AYP status by demonstrating significant growth on PPI. PPI was approved by the U.S. Department of Education in 2005 as an alternate AYP measure. If a school fails to meet its AMO targets for its student body in total and its subgroups, it can still meet AYP by hitting a target on PPI.

According to NCES, Pennsylvania's eighth grade assessment in math falls in the middle of a spectrum of states in terms of difficulty, well above Georgia's (NCES,

2007) (California was not one of the states in the eighth grade math comparison). Pennsylvania's eighth grade reading test seems to be quite rigorous compared with that of other states, just below California's test in difficulty but far above Georgia's test. The proficient levels on both exams correspond to NAEP scores between basic and proficient. Consistent with this evidence, Pennsylvania's AMO starting points in reading (45 percent) and math (35 percent) fall between California's and Georgia's (see Figures 2.1 and 2.2). Pennsylvania's AMO trajectory follows the same step pattern as Georgia's, but its trajectory is necessarily steeper given its lower AMO starting points. As with the other states in our study, Pennsylvania's AMO target increased during the middle year of our data collection but not in the other years we collected data.

In 2004–2005 and 2005–2006, Pennsylvania had roughly the same percentage of schools fail to make AYP as Georgia (about 20 percent). However, as noted earlier, Pennsylvania had fewer schools in improvement status than did Georgia (see Table 2.1).

Pennsylvania Findings from the ISBA Study

How Did Districts, Schools, and Teachers Respond to State Accountability Efforts, Including State Standards and State Tests?

Pennsylvania mathematics and science standards were perceived to be useful, but local curriculum was not always aligned with standards. Each year, about three-quarters of Pennsylvania mathematics teachers reported that the state standards were useful for planning their lessons (a somewhat smaller majority than in the other states we studied).[1] In comparison, only slightly more than one-half of Pennsylvania science teachers reported that the state standards were useful for planning their lessons in 2006, but this marked a 10 percentage-point increase from 2004. Although useful, the standards were perceived by many teachers as being too broad. In 2006, about two-thirds of mathematics and science teachers reported that the state standards included more content than could be adequately covered in a school year. This percentage had decreased among elementary mathematics teachers and increased among elementary science teachers from 2004 to 2006, suggesting growing comfort with the scope of elementary mathematics standards but not with the science standards. At the same time, about one-quarter of science teachers and a growing minority of mathematics teachers (from about 15 percent in 2004 to about one-quarter in 2006) reported that the standards omitted important topics that were part of their curriculum. Figure 4.1 shows that despite the fact that a majority of teachers found the standards useful, many teachers had concerns about the alignment of standards to their curriculum. Thus, in teachers' judgments, the standards may embody unrealistic expectations for how much content

---

[1]   The surveys administered in Pennsylvania asked about the "state standards and assessment anchors," which were considered part of the standards in that state.

Figure 4.1
Pennsylvania Teachers Agreeing with Statements About State Content Standards, 2006

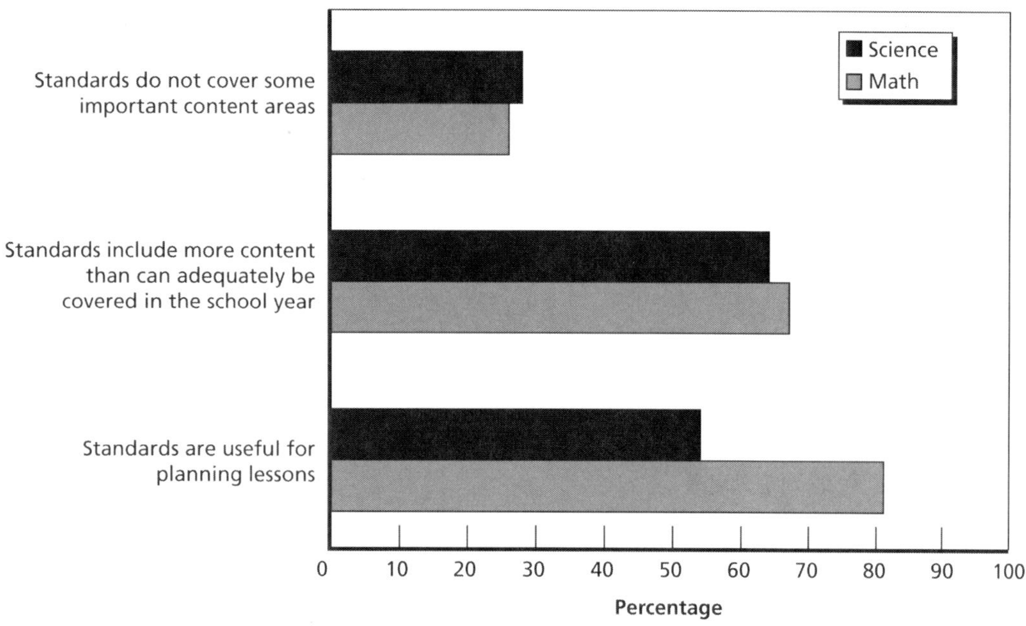

RAND *MG784-4.1*

can be covered, and there remains some misalignment between the content of the mathematics and science standards and the content of their curricula (see Tables B.1 and B.2).

A majority of educators did not believe that Pennsylvania mathematics and science assessments were good measures of student achievement. Administrators and teachers had mixed opinions about the quality of the state assessments. Each year, less than one-half of superintendents and middle school principals and just over one-half of elementary school principals thought that state assessments accurately reflected student achievement. These responses were generally lower than in the other states we studied. Similarly, in 2006 slightly fewer than half of mathematics teachers reported that the assessments were a good measure of students' mastery of content standards (although the percentage had increased from 2004 among elementary school teachers). Figure 4.2 shows that a majority of elementary school principals saw state assessments as valid indicators of student achievement but fewer middle school principals and teachers agreed. Furthermore, in 2006, about 40 percent of elementary mathematics teachers and about three-quarters of middle school mathematics teachers reported that the mathematics assessments were too difficult for their students, although these percentages had declined by 15 to 20 percentage points from 2004. Despite the introduction of the assessment anchors in the spring of 2004 for mathematics and reading, a substantial, although declining, minority of elementary mathematics teachers (from one-third in 2004 to under

Figure 4.2
Pennsylvania Educators Agreeing That States Assessment Scores Accurately Reflect Student Achievement (Principals) or Are Good Measures of Student Mastery (Teachers)

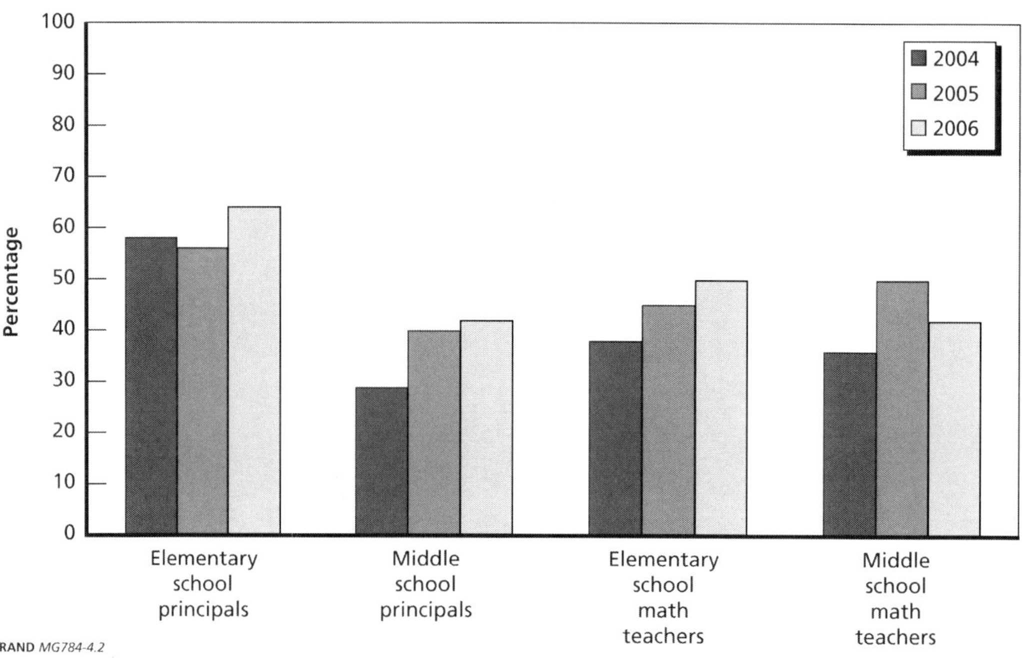

20 percent in 2006) and over one-third of middle school mathematics teachers reported that the state tests included content not in their curriculum, and similar percentages reported that the tests omitted content that was in their curriculum. As was the case with standards, some teachers perceive there to be misalignment between the content of the state assessments and the content of the local curriculum (see Tables B.3 and B.4).

Test results were widely available in a variety of formats, but they were not always available in a timely manner. Each year, almost all elementary school principals and over 80 percent of middle school principals reported that test results for the school as a whole, for student subgroups, and for content subtopics were available to them. Similarly, about 80 percent of mathematics teachers reported that test results were available to them by subgroup and by subtopic each year. However, educators gave mixed responses about the timeliness of test reporting. Fewer than one-quarter of principals reported receiving results in a timely manner in 2006 (similar to responses in previous years). The percentage of teachers reporting timely receipt of test reports declined from about two-thirds in 2004 to about one-half in 2006 (see Tables B.6 to B.10).

Test results were widely used by superintendents and principals, but teachers' reports of usefulness decreased from 2004 to 2006. Each year, two-thirds or more of superintendents reported that assessment results were helpful for each of the following purposes:

district and school planning, focusing PD, and curriculum reform. Similarly, two-thirds or more of principals said they found the test results useful for planning school improvement, focusing PD, reforming curriculum, and identifying students who need extra support. However, one-third or fewer of principals reported that the data were useful for making decisions regarding student promotion and retention and for identifying teachers' strengths and weaknesses (far fewer than in the other states we studied) (see Tables B.11 and B.12).

In 2006, about 60 percent of mathematics teachers said the test results were useful for identifying gaps in curriculum and instruction and for identifying areas where they needed to strengthen their content knowledge or teaching skills, down from about three-quarters in 2004. About 40 percent of mathematics teachers reported that the results were useful for tailoring instruction to individual student needs. Each year, just under one-third of the mathematics teachers said the subgroup results were useful to them, while about two-thirds of the mathematics teachers said the subtopic results were useful to them (see Tables B.13, B.8, and B.9).

Superintendents increasingly promoted the use of periodic progress tests[2] *in addition to the annual state test, and teachers found progress test results helpful for improving teaching and learning.* In 2005 and 2006, between one-third and two-thirds of superintendents reported that their districts required some or all elementary and middle schools to administer periodic progress tests to monitor student learning in mathematics; few superintendents required progress testing in science.[3] Progress test requirements in science were less common in Pennsylvania than in either of the two other states we studied, which is consistent with the fact that state testing in science was implemented later in Pennsylvania. Progress tests were typically administered either two to three times per year or every six to eight weeks, with a smaller number of teachers reporting more frequent testing. According to teachers, the use of progress tests in mathematics increased from 2004 to 2006; in 2006, over half of teachers reported that they were required to administer progress tests, up from about 30 percent of teachers in 2004. Each year, about 70 percent of teachers in schools that used progress tests reported that the progress test was a good measure of student mastery, and over 80 percent reported that the progress tests helped them identify and correct gaps in curriculum and instruction (both percentages are generally higher than the responses to comparable questions regarding the annual state tests) (see Tables B.14 to B.18). Figure 4.3 shows that a majority of teachers found both annual state tests and progress tests useful for identifying and correcting gaps in curriculum, but the percentage of elementary school and middle school teachers who found state tests useful for this purpose was

---

[2]   Progress tests are formal assessments given periodically during the year to measure student progress in mastering state standards. They are also called interim tests, formative tests, and benchmark tests. To our knowledge, these exams do not result in any consequences for teachers in the districts we studied.

[3]   We did not ask this question in 2004.

Figure 4.3
Pennsylvania Teachers Agreeing That Annual State Tests and Progress Tests Are Helpful in Identifying and Correcting Gaps in Curriculum and Instruction

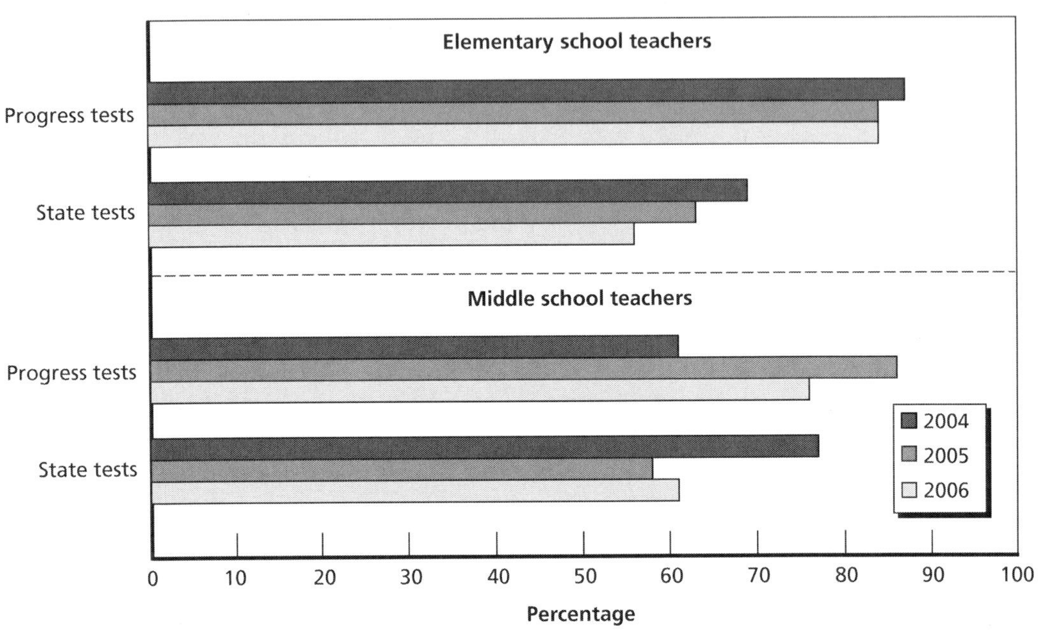

RAND *MG784-4.3*

decreasing over time, and the percentage of middle school teachers who found progress tests useful for this purpose was increasing over time.

Pennsylvania educators reported that they understood the state accountability system, but not all agreed that AYP status was a good reflection of their students' performance or that AYP targets would be attained in future years. Each year, almost all Pennsylvania administrators reported that they understood the AYP criteria being used in the state, and 80 percent or more of educators reported that they received help to understand all the accountability system requirements. On the other hand, a substantial, albeit declining, proportion of teachers reported that the system was too complicated to understand (slightly more than half in 2004 and about 40 percent in 2006). In 2004, only about one-third of superintendents and principals agreed that AYP status accurately reflected the overall performance of their students; but by 2006, over one-half of the administrators agreed. Principals in schools that made AYP were more likely to agree that AYP was an accurate reflection of student performance than principals in schools that did not. Each year, a majority of superintendents and middle school principals and almost all elementary school principals thought their schools or districts would make AYP the next year, but one-half or fewer believed they would continue to make AYP over the next five years (see Tables B.19 to B.23).

What School Improvement Strategies Were Used, and Which Were Perceived to Be Most Useful?

School improvement efforts incorporated a wide repertoire of strategies. Each year, seven of the strategies to improve school performance were reported to be used by two-thirds or more of principals, including matching curriculum and instruction with standards and/or assessments, using existing research, providing additional instruction to low-performing students, increasing the use of test data, increasing teacher PD, improving the school planning process, and providing out-of-school time programs. Less prevalent, but still common, were efforts to make the school more attractive to parents or to restructure the school day, with about half of principals reporting each of these strategies each year. About one-quarter of principals reported increasing instructional time by lengthening the school day or year or shortening recess (see Table B.24).

Data use, alignment, and focusing on low-performing students were the most important school improvement strategies, according to principals. In 2005, the three strategies identified as most important by the largest percentages of principals were increasing the use of achievement data to inform instruction (about one-half of elementary school principals and one-third of middle school principals), matching curriculum and instruction with standards and/or assessments (about 60 percent of all principals), and providing additional instruction to low-performing students (about one-half of elementary school principals and one-third of middle school principals). In 2006, these three strategies continued to be the ones reported as most important by the largest proportions of principals. Between 2005 and 2006, there was a 25 percentage-point increase in the proportion of middle schools principals who identified increasing use of achievement data as one of their three most important improvement strategies (see Table B.25).

Pennsylvania principals reported that their schools and districts engaged in a wide variety of test preparation activities. Each year, almost all principals reported that their schools were engaged in one or more forms of test preparation, including identifying content that is likely to appear on the state test, discussing methods for preparing students to take tests, and distributing released copies of the test or test items. In addition, about two-thirds of principals reported encouraging teachers to focus on students near the proficient level (bubble kids) in both 2005 and 2006 (see Table B.26).

According to superintendents, districts provided a range of support to principals and teachers for school improvement. In 2006, over 60 percent of districts implemented each of the following strategies to help schools align curriculum and instruction with standards in mathematics: establishing detailed curriculum guidelines aligned with state content standards, mapping the alignment of textbooks and instructional programs to state standards, and developing "pacing plans" or "instructional calendars" aligned with standards.[4] Generally smaller proportions of districts made similar alignment

---

[4] These questions were not asked in 2004.

efforts in science. Each year, about 80 percent of mathematics teachers reported that the district actions listed above were useful to them in aligning their curriculum (see Tables B.27 to B.30).

Each year, over 60 percent of principals reported that their districts provided needed assistance to schools when they were having difficulties, appropriate support to enable principals to act as instructional leaders, and appropriate instructional support for teachers. In 2006, about 90 percent of superintendents reported that their districts helped some or all schools obtain additional PD to apply the results of scientifically based research about education, up from about two-thirds in 2004. Each year, 30 percent or more of superintendents reported assigning additional full-time school-level staff to support teacher development in some or all schools, and 15 percent or more provided a coach or mentor to assist the principal in some or all schools. Also, 85 percent or more of districts helped some or all schools analyze assessment data to identify and address problems in instruction. Most superintendents reported providing guidance for teaching grade-level standards to ELLs and/or special education students, assisting schools in implementing proven instructional strategies, and providing before- or after-school, weekend, or summer programs. Technical assistance was typically offered to all schools, not just those that were low performing (see Tables B.31 and B.32).

Superintendents also reported that districts intervened and required schools to take certain actions to improve student performance. For example, in both 2005 and 2006 almost all districts required some or all elementary schools to offer remedial assistance to students outside the normal school day,[5] and over 80 percent required the same of middle schools. Also in both years, about one-half of districts required schools to increase the amount of instruction that low-achieving students received in mathematics, but few required increased time for low-achieving students in science. In addition, some districts required schools to implement a new mathematics or science curriculum. Each year, about one-third of districts required middle schools to implement new math curricula, and about one-third required elementary schools to do the same. Similar proportions of districts required their schools to implement new science curricula (see Tables B.33 to B.35).

In 2006, there were only nine schools (from a sample of 97) identified for improvement in our sample, so our estimates of responses from identified schools are not as precise as our estimates from all schools. However, in these schools the most common forms of district or state assistance were additional PD resources and special grants to support school improvement. There were only four schools in corrective action in our sample in 2006 (see Tables B.36 and B.37).

PD emphasized aligning curriculum and instruction with standards, as well as other improvement strategies. Across all three years, about 60 percent of teachers reported that aligning curriculum and instruction with standards was a major emphasis of the PD

---

[5]   We did not ask this question in 2004.

they received. Other topics that received strong emphasis from more than one-half of teachers each year were preparing students to take state assessments, and mathematics and mathematics teaching. About 40 percent of teachers reported an emphasis on instructional strategies for low-achieving students, and about one-third of teachers said that PD had a major focus on interpreting and using student test results (see Table B.38).

Districts that reported needing technical assistance from the state often did not receive it. In 2005 and 2006, over three-quarters of districts reported that they needed technical assistance to identify research-based instructional strategies, provide effective PD, and use data more effectively.[6] However, only about 40 to 60 percent of superintendents who needed technical assistance in these areas reported that they received the assistance they needed (a level that was lower than in the other states we studied). Similarly, one-third to one-half of the districts that needed technical assistance in other areas in 2006 (e.g., clarifying accountability system rules and requirements, developing curriculum guides or model lessons, promoting parent involvement, or working with schools in need of improvement) reported that they received it. The reported receipt of technical assistance to develop district improvement plans dropped from about 70 percent in 2005 to about 20 percent in 2006 (see Table B.39).

What Was the Impact of Accountability on Curriculum, Teacher Practice, and Student Learning?

Most principals thought the accountability system had positive effects on curriculum and instruction, but teachers' responses were not as positive. Each year, more than half of elementary school principals but slightly fewer than half of middle school principals thought the academic rigor of the curriculum had improved because of accountability. Teachers were less sanguine than principals, about 30 percent reporting that academic rigor had changed for the better, and about 20 percent reporting that it changed for the worse; these teacher responses were more negative than responses from teachers in the other states we studied. Figure 4.4 shows that in each year, teachers were much less likely than administrators to report that the academic rigor of the curriculum had improved. Similarly, in 2006 about two-thirds of principals reported changes for the better in students' learning of important skills and knowledge, but fewer than one-third of teachers agreed, and 15 percent of middle school teachers thought changes had been for the worse. These percentages represent increases from 2004, in particular among middle school principals. In addition, in 2006 over two-thirds of principals reported that teachers' focus on student learning had changed for the better as a result of the state accountability system, but only about 40 percent of teachers concurred (responses were similar in 2004). In fact, in 2004, over 15 percent of teachers reported

---

[6]   We did not ask this question in 2004.

Figure 4.4
Pennsylvania Educators Agreeing That the Academic Rigor of the Curriculum Had Improved as a Result of Accountability

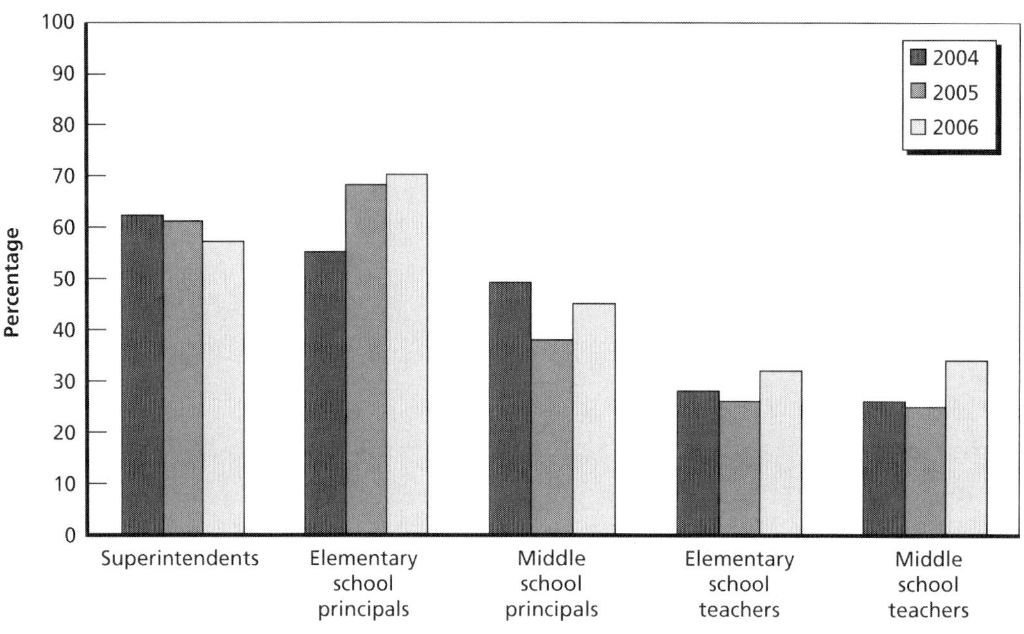

RAND *MG784-4.4*

that the focus on student learning had actually changed for the worse as a result of the accountability system, though this declined to fewer than 10 percent by 2006. Overall, about two-thirds of principals but less than one-third of teachers reported each year that the state's accountability system was beneficial for students (see Tables B.40 and B.41).

Each year, about 35 to 40 percent of teachers reported that their teaching practices had changed for the better as a result of the accountability system, although fewer than 20 percent thought their relations with their students had improved, as well. Sixty percent or more of elementary school math teachers and a growing majority of middle school math teachers (from just over half in 2004 to three-quarters in 2006) reported that the state tests had led them to search for more effective teaching methods. Two-thirds to three-quarters of middle schools teachers but only 15 to 20 percent of elementary school teachers reported that they offered more assistance outside of the school day to students who were not proficient as a result of the accountability system (see Tables B.42 to B.44).

In 2006, almost all superintendents and about two-thirds of principals reported that coordination of the mathematics curricula across grades had changed for the better as a result of accountability, but only about 60 percent of superintendents and 40 percent of principals reported improved coordination of the curricula in science (these percentages represented an increase from 2004 among superintendents). In contrast, about 70 percent of teachers reported that staff morale had changed for the worse as a result of the accountability system in 2004, although that percentage had declined slightly to about 60 percent by 2006 (see Figure 4.5 and Tables B.45 and B.46).

Teachers responded to standards-based accountability by aligning their curricula and instruction with standards and assessments, but did not report changing specific teaching techniques. Teachers reported making a lot of changes in curricula and instruction in response to standards-based accountability. Perhaps the most widespread change involved aligning curricula and instruction with standards and assessments. Each year, over three-quarters of mathematics teachers reported that they had aligned their instruction with the standards, and over 80 percent also reported aligning instruction with state assessments (see Table B.47).

Teachers reported that their focus on alignment was due, in part, to the test-based accountability system. Each year, about three-quarters of elementary school math teachers and over half of middle school math teachers reported that they focused more on standards as a result of the state testing program. Over 70 percent of elementary school math teachers and just under half of middle school math teachers also reported that as a result of the state assessment, they focused more on covered topics and placed more emphasis on question styles and formats from the test (see Tables B.43 and B.44).

Figure 4.5
Pennsylvania Educators Agreeing That Staff Morale Had Changed for the Worse as a Result of Accountability

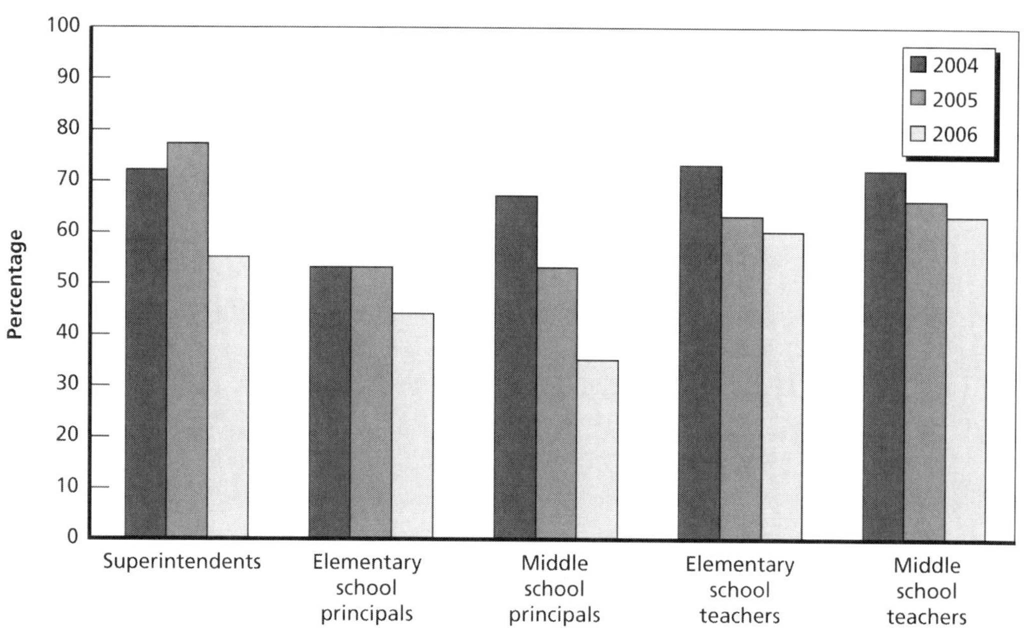

It appears that teachers' efforts to improve alignment did not typically involve changing the amount of time devoted to specific subjects. Each year, over 60 percent of teachers reported no changes in the amount of time students spent on each of the following subjects: mathematics, reading/language arts, science, social studies, arts and music, and physical education. Only about one-quarter to one-third of elementary school teachers and 10 to 20 percent of middle school teachers reported increasing the time they spent on mathematics and reading/language arts each year, and few reported decreasing time on these two subjects. However, about one-quarter of elementary school teachers reported decreasing the time spent on science or social studies each year. It is important to note that we asked teachers about changes over the past year in the amount of time allocated to subjects. As a result, teachers' responses would not be expected to reflect cumulative changes since the enactment of NCLB. Thus, it is possible that these findings underestimate the amount of time reallocated between subjects as a result of NCLB accountability provisions (see Tables B.48 and B.49).

In general, elementary and middle school mathematics and science teachers' reports about particular teaching techniques were similar from 2005 to 2006. Almost all mathematics teachers and smaller majorities of science teachers reported that they sometimes or often used each of the following techniques included in the survey: introducing content through formal presentations or direct instruction, assigning homework, having students help other students learn content, reteaching topics because performance did not meet expectations, and reviewing assessment results to identify individual students who needed supplemental instruction or to identify topics requiring more or less emphasis in instruction. In contrast, fewer than one-half of mathematics teachers reported having students work on extended mathematics investigations or projects, but over three-quarters of science teachers reported having their student do hands-on laboratory activities or investigations (see Tables B.50 to B.53).

About half of teachers were concerned that the strong focus on test scores deprived high-achieving students of a challenging curriculum. Slightly more than one-half of middle school teachers and slightly less than one-half of elementary school teachers reported in 2005 and 2006 that high-achieving students were not receiving an appropriately challenging curriculum as a result of the accountability system.[7] Other survey responses offer possible explanations for this concern. Each year, over 80 percent of teachers felt that the accountability system left little time to teach material that is not on the state test. This can be viewed as a positive outcome given that SBA is designed to ensure that students master the content outlined in state standards and measured by the assessments. However, this narrow focus on the standards may exclude teaching advanced material that could benefit high-achieving students. Each year, about one-quarter of mathematics teachers said the state tests caused them to focus more on students near the proficient level (bubble kids) than they would have absent the test (perhaps at the

---

[7]   We did not ask this question in 2004.

expense of students farther to the extremes of the achievement spectrum) (see Tables B.54, B.43, and B.44).

What Conditions Hindered Improvement Efforts?

Inadequate funding, inadequate materials, and insufficient time were reported to hinder efforts to improve performance. Resources are always a concern in education, and each year over 80 percent of superintendents reported that lack of adequate funding was a moderate to great hindrance to their improvement efforts. Each year about three-quarters of middle school principals and over half of elementary school principals concurred. School facilities were less of a concern; in 2006, fewer than 20 percent of superintendents and elementary school principals (but more than one-third of middle school principals) reported that inadequate school facilities impeded improvement efforts (responses were similar in previous years). Thirty percent or more of superintendents said shortages of standards-based curriculum materials were a problem each year. Teachers reported similar judgments; one-quarter to one-third of teachers reported that inadequate instructional materials hindered students' academic success each year (see Tables B.55 and B.56).

Shortages of time for planning, administration, and instruction were other factors that were reported to hinder improvement efforts. In 2006, about 60 percent of elementary school principals and about 40 percent of middle school principals (down from about 60 percent in 2005)[8] reported that they had insufficient staff time to perform their administrative duties. Each year, over half of Pennsylvania teachers reported that there was insufficient class time to cover the curriculum, and about one-half of elementary school teachers and about 30 percent of middle school teachers reported that there was inadequate planning time built into the school day. Responses from principals were similar; in 2006, about 40 percent of elementary school principals and 20 percent of middle school principals reported that lack of teacher planning time was a hindrance to school improvement (responses were similar in 2005)[9] (see Tables B.57 to B.59).

Teachers reported that large class sizes and a wide range of student abilities in class were hindrances to student academic success. Each year, about three-quarters of teachers reported that the wide range of student abilities they had to address in class was a hindrance to students' academic success. Similarly, about half of teachers reported that large class sizes hindered students' academic success in 2006 (slightly lower than in 2004) (see Table B.60 and B.56).

Reported district capacity to support school improvement decreased between 2004 and 2006. Superintendents' responses indicated that fewer districts had the staff capacity to provide school support in 2006 than in 2004. In 2004, 80 percent of districts or

---

[8]   We did not ask this question in 2004.

[9]   We did not ask this question in 2004.

more reported adequate capacity to facilitate improvement in low-performing schools, help schools analyze data for school improvement, help schools identify research-based strategies for improvement, and align curriculum with state content standards and state assessments. However, by 2006 these proportions had dropped to 30 to 45 percent of districts. This pattern is in stark contrast to California and Georgia, where reported staff capacity typically increased over the three years from already high levels in 2004 (see Table B.61).

Some districts and schools were hindered by shortages of highly qualified principals and highly qualified mathematics and science teachers, and one-half of districts or fewer were hindered by a lack of high-quality PD opportunities for principals and teachers. A shortage of human capital was a concern for superintendents and principals, as well. Each year, 20 to 30 percent of superintendents reported a lack of qualified principals, and about 20 percent of middle school principals reported a lack of highly qualified teachers. Shortages of qualified mathematics and science teachers hindered efforts to improve performance in 30 to 40 percent of districts. In addition, one-third to one-half of superintendents reported each year that their improvement efforts were hindered by shortages of high-quality PD opportunities for principals and for teachers. About one-half of middle school principals also reported a lack of high-quality PD opportunities for teachers in 2004 and 2006 (there was an unexplained dip in 2005). The percentage of elementary school principals reporting a lack of high-quality PD opportunities for both principals and teachers doubled between 2004 and 2006, from about 15 percent to about one-third. Shortages of qualified aides or paraprofessionals were a problem for about 15 to 30 percent of principals each year (see Table B.57).

Most teachers reported that lack of parental support and students' lack of basic skills impeded their efforts to improve student achievement. Each year, about 70 percent of elementary school teachers and 80 percent of middle school teachers reported that their efforts to improve student achievement were hindered by lack of support from parents, while over 60 percent of elementary school teachers and over 80 percent of middle school teachers reported that inadequate basic skills or prior preparation was a hindrance. In 2006, most elementary school and middle school teachers reported that inadequate basic skills or prior preparation and lack of support from parents were hindrances to students' academic success (see Figure 4.6). In addition, student absenteeism and tardiness were concerns for half of the elementary school teachers and over 70 percent of the middle school teachers each year (see Table B.60).

Administrators reported that changes in state policies and state leadership, as well as compliance with teacher association rules, were impediments to improvement. Administrative concerns hindered some superintendents and principals in their efforts to improve performance. Each year, more than two-thirds of superintendents said frequent changes in state policy or leadership were hindrances to improvement. Superintendent reports that complying with teacher association rules or policies hindered their improvement efforts increased from about 40 percent in 2004 to 70 percent

Figure 4.6
Pennsylvania Teachers Reporting That Selected Conditions Were Moderate or Great Hindrances to Students' Academic Success

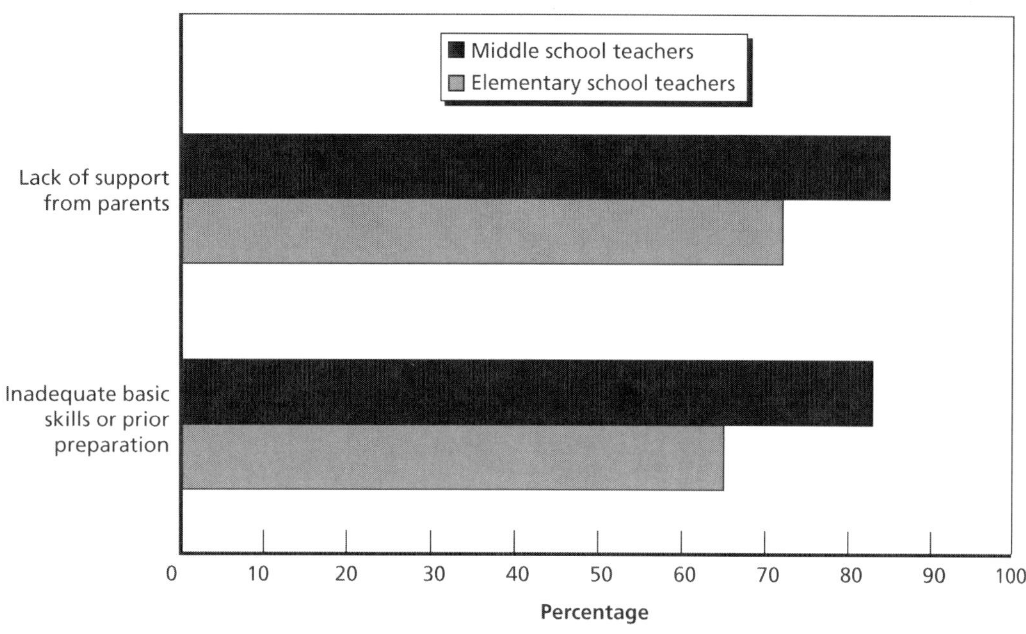

RAND *MG784-4.6*

in 2006. In 2006, about one-quarter of superintendents reported that disagreements with district school boards over policies hindered their improvement efforts (up from fewer than 10 percent in 2004). Some principals said frequent changes in district policy or district leadership hindered their improvement efforts (see Table B.62).

Some principals reported that a lack of guidance for teaching special-needs populations was a hindrance to their school improvement efforts. In 2005 and 2006, about one-quarter of elementary school principals and between 20 and 40 percent of middle school principals reported that a lack of guidance for teaching standards to special education students (i.e., students in IEPs) was a moderate or great hindrance to their school improvement efforts. Between 15 and 30 percent of elementary school principals and 20 percent or fewer middle school principals cited the same concern in reference to ELLs (see Table B.63).

CHAPTER FIVE

Conclusions

Although this study examined only three states, we think the results can be valuable to educators and policymakers concerned with the implementation of No Child Left Behind, in particular, and the application of standards-based accountability, in general. First, we observed common responses across districts and schools in California, Georgia, and Pennsylvania that may generalize to other states. Respondents had strong opinions about NCLB itself, steps that were taken to implement it, and its impact on their practices. Understanding these reactions from the field can be beneficial in thinking about how to achieve the goals of the existing legislation and improve future authorizations of the law. Second, in some cases, educators' responses changed consistently during the three years of the study. Where clear trends appeared, we can make inferences about dynamic features of implementation to help set expectations for future growth or decline. Third, there were some notable differences in responses among the three states. Although these differences cannot always be fully explained in terms of the elements of state context that we measured, context can often be used to relate results from this study to other states. The following paragraphs discuss these three types of conclusions based on evidence from California, Georgia, and Pennsylvania during the period 2004 to 2006. We will not review every finding from the study, but we will draw attention to issues that have arisen in other research on NCLB and themes that might be of particular interest for future efforts to design and implement standards based accountability. Where appropriate, we compare results of this study with findings from recent research on the implementation of NCLB, including results from the National Longitudinal Study of No Child Left Behind (U.S. Department of Education, 2007a and 2007b) and a series of studies conducted by the Center on Education Policy (CEP, 2006, 2007a, 2007b, and 2008).

Common Themes Across the Three States

States, Districts, and Schools Have Adapted Their Policies and Practices to Support the Implementation of NCLB

Although these changes took a few years, by the end of this study, all three states had constructed most of the infrastructure needed to support standards-based account-ability, including academic standards, aligned assessments, reporting mechanisms, and support structures. This finding is consistent with national reports that all states had adopted academic standards and were making progress in implementing the required tests by 2005–2006 (U.S. Department of Education, 2007b, pp. 10–11). Further-more, educators in all three states were familiar with federal rules as implemented in their states; they appeared to understand the language of the reform, the policies that affected them directly, and the responsibilities that were theirs.

Alignment Was a Major Focus of Efforts to Implement NCLB

Efforts were made at all levels—state, district, school, and classroom—to ensure consis-tency among the standards, assessments, curriculum, and instruction. There were some false starts (e.g., Georgia's initial standards were judged to be insufficiently rigorous; Pennsylvania's initial standards lacked the level of detail teachers wanted), but states responded with changes to address those shortcomings. Not surprisingly, alignment was a major focus of implementation efforts across the country, as well. Forty-nine states reported that their strategies to raise student achievement relied either moder-ately or to a great extent on having curriculum and instruction aligned with stan-dards and/or assessments (CEP, 2007b, p. 9). Over 70 percent of schools nationwide reported that aligning curriculum and instruction with standards and/or assessments was a major focus of their school improvement efforts (U.S. Department of Education, 2007b, p. 88).

Despite all these efforts, misalignment remains a concern among a minority of teachers in these three states. Teachers reported that both standards and assessments exclude some topics that are part of their local curriculum and include some topics that are not. Figure 5.1 shows that although a majority of math and science teachers in each state found the standards useful for planning lessons, many teachers were concerned that the standards either included too much content or omitted important content. Such misalignment might occur because textbook adoptions occur infrequently and some districts have not yet caught up, because old materials are still in use, or because teachers or administrators are reluctant to change a curriculum that they endorse and/ or find familiar.

Similar alignment challenges have been reported in national studies. For exam-ple, while 90 percent of teachers nationwide reported that they had access to district or school content standards to augment the state standards, only 47 percent had access to detailed information showing the alignment of required textbooks and instructional

Figure 5.1
Teachers Agreeing with Statements About State Academic Standards, 2006

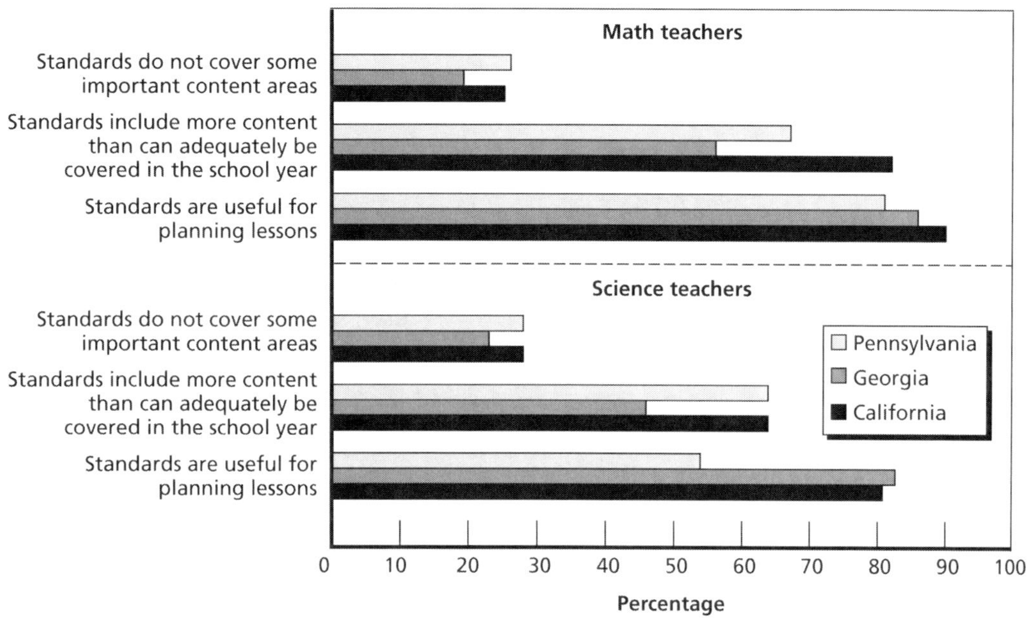

programs to state standards (U.S. Department of Education, 2007b, p. 90). Eighteen percent of teachers said that having textbooks that are not aligned with state standards was a moderate or major challenge to improving student performance (U.S. Department of Education, 2007b, p. 91).

Educators Think That Test Results Are a Good Measure of Student Mastery and Provide Useful Information for Improving Curriculum and Instruction

Despite some reported mismatches between testing and curriculum, most administrators and many teachers in all three states report that test results provide a good measure of student mastery, i.e., they are confident in the quality of the information provided by the tests. Confidence in the value of test results can also be inferred from the widespread adoption in these three states of periodic progress tests to monitor instruction more frequently. In fact, progress tests are becoming far more common across the country; two-thirds of schools reported supplementing annual state tests with progress assessments (U.S. Department of Education, 2007b, p. 97). Teachers in California, Georgia, and Pennsylvania schools that adopted progress tests agree that those tests are good measures of student mastery, as well.

Teachers also report that the information they obtain from student tests is useful for identifying and correcting gaps in curriculum and instruction. This finding is consistent with national reports of efforts to use achievement data for school improvement.

For example, 82 percent of identified schools and 67 percent of nonidentified schools said that using data to inform instruction was a major focus of their school improvement efforts (U.S. Department of Education, 2007b, p. 88). In fact, teachers in schools that use progress tests were more likely to report that progress tests were useful for identifying and correcting gaps in curriculum and instruction than teachers in all schools were to report that annual state tests were useful for these purposes.

Most Educators Report That NCLB Has Had a Positive Impact on Teaching and Learning, Although Concerns Remain About Potential Negative Effects on Some Students

Almost all administrators and most teachers in California, Georgia, and Pennsylvania agreed that state academic standards were useful guides and that standards-based accountability had led to certain improvements in instruction. In particular, educators in these three states felt that NCLB had led teachers to focus more on student learning and had resulted in improvement in the academic rigor of the curriculum. CEP (2007b, p. 2) reports that educators think the NCLB interventions for low-performing schools—such as extending the day, assigning outside experts, or implementing new curriculum—are effective, as well.

However, many teachers raised concerns that the system was not serving all students equally well. For example, many thought that NCLB led teachers to focus on the bubble kids—those near the proficient level (perhaps at the expense of students who had farther to go to reach proficiency). As can be seen in Figure 5.2, the percentage of elementary school math teachers who reported that they focused more on students who were close to proficient as a result of the state math assessment increased over time in each of the three states we studied (although the change was not statistically significant in Pennsylvania). In addition, some teachers reported that high-achieving students were not receiving appropriately challenging curriculum and instruction.

Despite the Changes in Alignment and Instructional Planning, It Appears That Teaching Techniques Have Generally Not Changed

Teachers in California, Georgia, and Pennsylvania reported many changes that relate to instruction (e.g., aligning the content of lessons with the standards, using test results to make instructional plans), but they did not appear to have made changes in their regular interactions with students (e.g., direct instruction, use of peer coaching). The evidence we collected suggests that teachers were not changing their day-to-day instructional techniques in response to NCLB. This finding is interesting in light of national reports that most districts are providing training to help teachers change their teaching techniques to be more effective. In one national study, over 60 percent of districts reported that they were training teachers to use specific methods to address the academic needs of low-performing subgroups of students in either reading or mathematics (CEP, 2007b, p. 25). Our surveys may not have been sensitive to these particular

Figure 5.2
Elementary School Teachers Reporting That They Focused More on Students Near Proficiency in Mathematics as a Result of State Mathematics Assessments

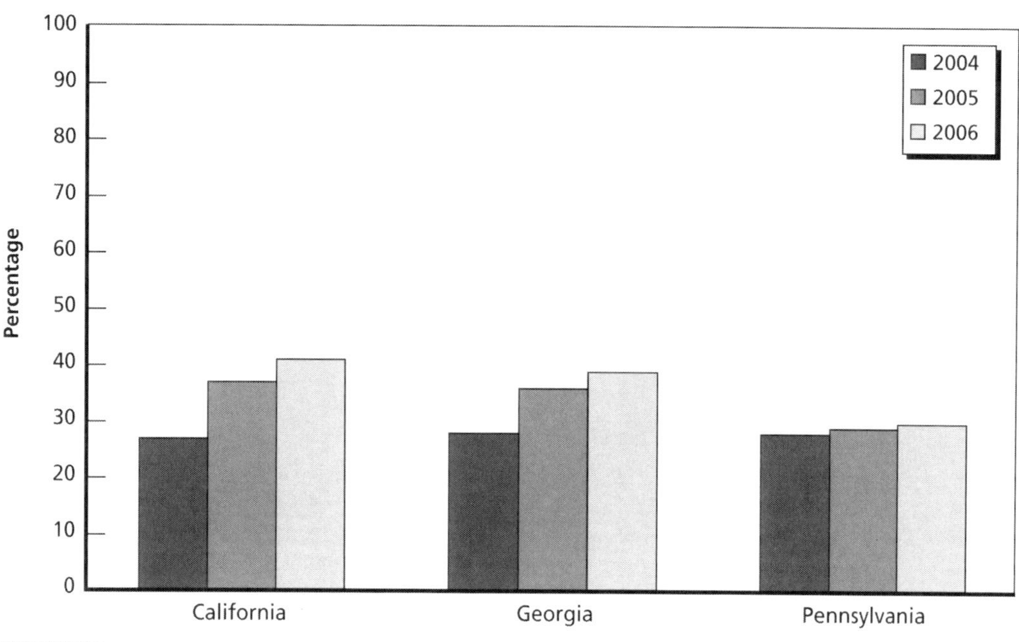

RAND *MG784-5.2*

efforts, or districts in these states may not have been typical of the nation; however, it would be wise to explore further the actual impact of districts' PD efforts on teachers' instructional practices.

Teachers Are Less Sanguine Than Administrators About the Validity of Test Scores and the Impact of NCLB on Students

In all three states, teachers were more likely than administrators to find fault with the state tests and to worry about the impact of the reform on certain students. For example, fewer teachers than administrators thought the tests were good measures of student performance, and many teachers reported that the tests were too difficult for their students. Figure 5.3 shows that in 2006, a smaller proportion of teachers than either district administrators or school principals thought that state exams were valid indicators of student achievement. As can be seen in Figure 5.4, principals were generally more likely than were teachers to think that the accountability system overall had been beneficial for students. Our case study interviews suggest that teachers were acutely aware of the problems some students had performing well on state tests, and they may be less optimistic in their judgments as a result. Administrators, who are farther from the classroom, may be less attuned to these specific concerns.

Figure 5.3
Educators Agreeing That State Assessment Scores Accurately Reflect Student Achievement (Administrators) or Are Good Measures of Student Mastery (Teachers), 2006

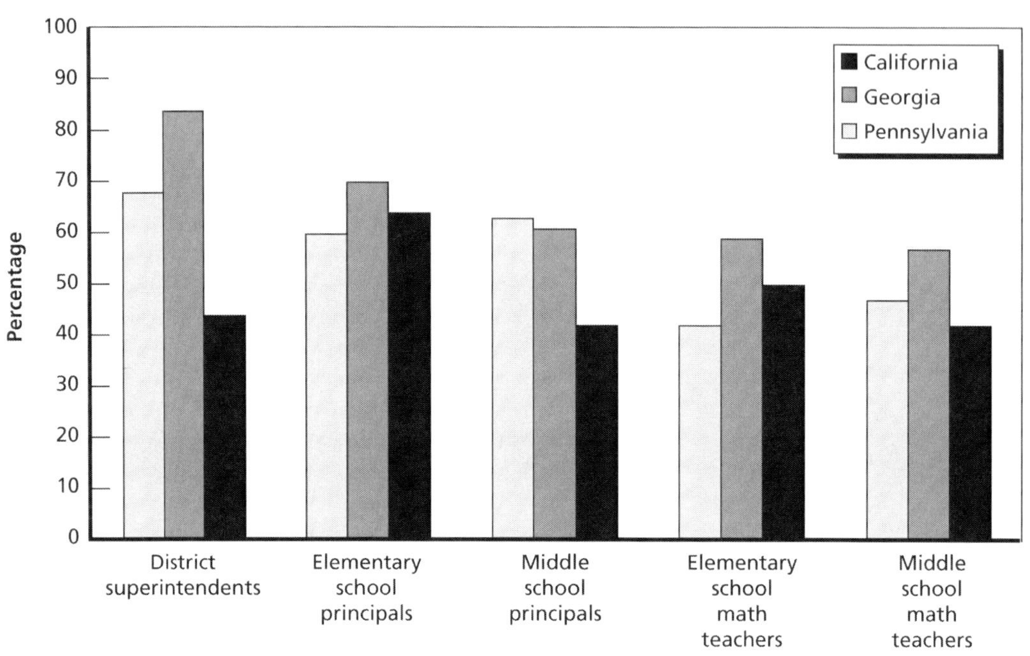

Districts and Schools Are Engaged in a Wide Variety of Reforms

Superintendents and principals reported making many changes in efforts to improve performance. The most attention has been paid to alignment, focusing on low-performing students, and using test results. Yet, almost every strategy included in the survey was endorsed by a majority of respondents. This multifaceted approach to school improvement is consistent with national reports that nearly all schools are making many improvement efforts. For example, more than half of the principals reported placing a major emphasis on nine of the ten improvement strategies included in the National Longitudinal Study of the NCLB school survey (U.S. Department of Education, 2007b, p. 88).

There Are Small but Notable Differences in Implementation Between Elementary and Middle Schools

In this study, as in other studies of NCLB, there were a number of differences in responses associated with school level. For example, elementary schools in California, Georgia, and Pennsylvania were more likely than middle schools to implement progress tests and to be required to implement a new curriculum. The first finding is consistent with the National Longitudinal Study of NCLB, which found that 76 percent

Figure 5.4
Educators Agreeing That State's Accountability System Has Been Beneficial for Students, 2006

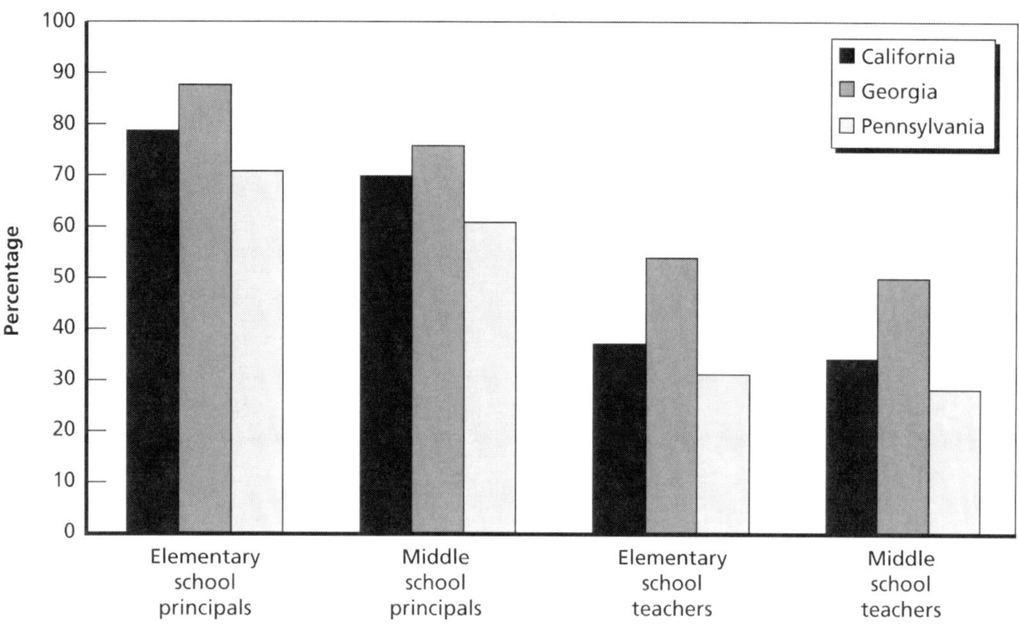

RAND *MG784-5.4*

of elementary schools were administering progress tests in reading compared with 57 percent of middle schools and only 48 percent of high schools (U.S. Department of Education, 2007b, p. 98). Elementary school teachers in the current study were more likely than middle school teachers to receive PD that focused on the use of test results. By comparison, the National Longitudinal Study did not find big differences in the amount of PD focusing on mathematics and reading instruction that was received by elementary and secondary teachers (U.S. Department of Education, 2007a, p. 72). Yet, CEP (2007b, pp. 19–20) reported that districts were more likely to use selected improvement strategies—including increasing the amount of PD—with identified elementary schools than with identified secondary schools. Furthermore, in two of the three states, a higher proportion of elementary school teachers than middle school teachers increased the time they devoted to mathematics in each of the three years we studied. We hypothesize, as did the authors of the CEP report, that some of these differences can be attributed to the fact that schedules are typically less flexible in secondary schools, where students have different teachers for each subject. It is also interesting to note that elementary school principals in California, Georgia, and Pennsylvania were more likely than middle school principals to believe their school would make AYP over the next five years.

There Are Major Differences in Implementation Between the Subjects of Mathematics and Science

The NCLB guidelines give states more time to implement science standards and tests than mathematics or reading standards and tests,[1] require science testing at fewer grade levels than mathematics and reading testing, and do not include science results in determining a school's AYP. As a result, in California, Georgia, and Pennsylvania far more effort has been made to implement standards-based accountability in mathematics than in science. This finding is illustrated by the fact that fewer schools report aligning their science programs with standards, implementing a new science curriculum, allocating more time to science instruction, or providing PD for teaching science. While not surprising given the NCLB requirements, this pattern is worthy of note because it illustrates an important feature of standards-based accountability: Subjects that do not "count" as much do not command resources or attention.[2]

Administrative Efforts Were Hindered by Lack of Funding and Lack of Time; Instructional Efforts Were Hindered by Lack of Time, Large and Heterogeneous Classes, and Poor Student Preparation

Meeting the expectations of NCLB has proven to be a challenging task, and educators in California, Georgia, and Pennsylvania highlighted a number of factors that hinder their progress. Both superintendents and principals reported that inadequate funding presents an obstacle to improvement. They also complained that administrative staff has inadequate time to perform all their duties. Time was also a concern when it comes to instruction. Most teachers said there is inadequate class time to cover the curriculum, and about half said they also lack adequate planning time during the day. Teachers also reported that their efforts are hampered by the large number of students in their classes and the wide range of student abilities they have to address. Finally, teachers were concerned that their students lack basic skills (that they should have learned previously) and that they do not receive adequate support from parents. Some of these concerns echo findings from a CEP case study of restructuring schools in California; many respondents reported that schools' efforts to raise achievement were hampered by factors outside of their control (CEP, 2008, p. 2).

---

[1]   States did not have to implement science tests until 2007–2008, the year after our third round of surveys.

[2]   It is worth noting that California's own accountability system did include science results, although science counted for only a small percentage of a school's score.

Trends

Patterns based on three years of data can only cautiously be interpreted as trends. Nevertheless, it is interesting to note the following instances in which we found consistently increasing or decreasing reports during the study period.

State Infrastructure for Accountability Has Improved

According to reports from administrators and teachers, the departments of education in these three states were generally becoming more efficient with their assessment and reporting systems, providing information more quickly or in more diverse ways. This finding is consistent with national reports that found that states were improving their data systems during this period (U.S. Department of Education, 2007b, p. 65). Improved data systems are one of the ways in which the impact of the law continued to "broaden and deepen" during this period (CEP, 2006, p. vii). While there were also some improvements at the local level (e.g., fewer reports of shortages of aligned curricula, inadequate facilities, or inadequate funding), local conditions were static in many districts in California, Georgia, and Pennsylvania.

State Reporting of Test Results Has Become Timelier and More Complete

Despite some problems with test administration in Georgia and the implementation of new examinations in Pennsylvania, the reporting of test results has generally improved over this time period. Growing percentages of elementary school respondents in all three states (and secondary school respondents in Georgia) said that test results were being provided in a more timely manner, or that they had access to subgroups or subtopic data, or both. Again, this finding matches national findings that states were improving the timeliness of their performance reports during this period (U.S. Department of Education, 2007b, p. 64–65).

The Use of Progress Tests Is Growing, as Are Efforts to Use Test Results for Instructional Decisionmaking

Increasing proportions of educators reported that periodic progress assessments were being administered to students so teachers would have more frequent and immediate data to use for instructional planning. Figure 5.5 shows that in each state the percentage of math teachers who reported that they were required to administer progress tests increased from 2004 to 2006 (although the changes from 2004 to 2006 were not always statistically significant). Also, teachers were more likely to report that the results from such progress tests were useful to them than the results from annual state assessments. This growth is consistent with a growing emphasis on data-driven decisionmaking as a school improvement tool (Marsh, Pane, and Hamilton, 2006). Our longitudinal study allows us to monitor growth more closely than the national studies of NCLB implementation, but these findings are consistent with the prominence of progress tests

Figure 5.5
Teachers Required to Administer Mathematics Progress Tests

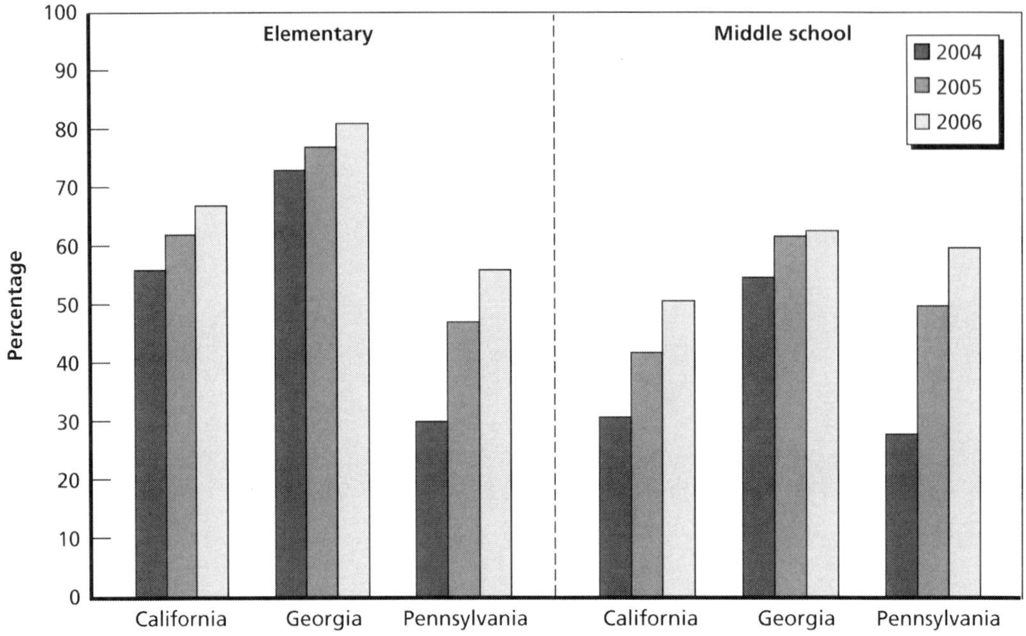

RAND *MG784-5.5*

and efforts to promote the use of test data for improvement that have been reported nationally (CEP, 2007b; U.S. Department of Education, 2007b). Neither this study nor the national studies offer much evidence about the success of such efforts, but they are generally endorsed by teachers and administrators in these three states.

Educators Are Growing More Positive Toward Accountability Policies

Growing proportions of educators in the three states reported that accountability has improved the academic rigor of the curriculum and increased the school's focus on student learning. During this period, teachers were also more likely to report that their own teaching had improved as a result of accountability (although these gains were not always statistically significant and there were no changes over time in their reported use of specific teaching practices).

Concerns About Low Morale Continue, but Are Becoming Less Common

Educators in these three states raised concerns about the negative effects of accountability, particularly its impact on teacher morale. This finding is consistent with CEP reports from several districts that "NCLB has escalated pressure on teachers to a stressful level and has negatively affected staff morale in some schools" (CEP, 2006, p. 1). Yet, the prevalence of these concerns in California, Georgia, and Pennsylvania declined during the period of this study, as can be seen clearly in Figure 5.6. We cannot say

Figure 5.6
Teachers Agreeing That Staff Morale Has Changed for the Worse as a Result of Accountability

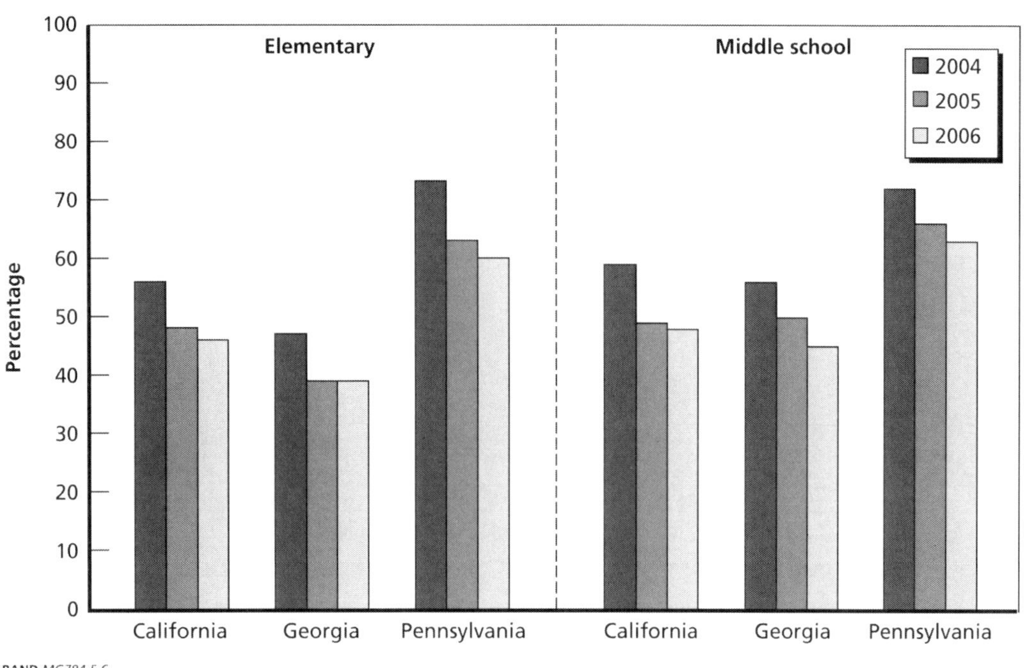

whether the decline reflects positive changes in the environment or readjustment on the part of respondents, but it is certainly a welcome development.

Distinctive Approaches by States

We also observed differences in NCLB implementation among the states in a number of areas. These differences may be explained, in part, by three facts. First, the states set very different levels for proficiency. We did not observe this directly, but using NAEP as a yardstick, other researchers have established that there are substantial differences among these three states in the difficulty of the proficiency cutoff point (U.S. Department of Education, 2007b, p. 19). The Georgia standard for proficiency is less rigorous than the Pennsylvania standard, which is, in turn, less rigorous than the California standard (NCES, 2007). One consequence of the differences in proficiency levels is that the percentage of proficient students is much greater in Georgia than in the other states. This translates into differences in AMO starting points for schools and differences in annual gains required to stay on target. As a result, meeting annual targets may be easier in Georgia than in Pennsylvania or California. A second factor is that Georgia is a "right to work" state, and teacher unions are not a strong presence in relations between teachers and school districts. Third, California has a more diverse student population than the other two states, and more-heterogeneous schools must meet more targets under NCLB and tend to make AYP at lower rates. These are just three of many context and policy differences among the states. With this background in mind, we highlight a few state-level differences.

States Varied in Their Capacity to Implement NCLB

NCLB has placed additional demands on states, and many lack the capacity to respond. According to a 2006 national study, 36 states did not have enough staff to implement NCLB, and 33 states found that federal funds were inadequate to assist all schools that were identified for improvement (CEP, 2006, pp. ix–x). California, Georgia, and Pennsylvania differed in a number of ways that influenced their capacity to implement NCLB and to support district and school improvement. Pennsylvania had a strong tradition of local control and a relatively decentralized education system prior to 2001. The Pennsylvania Department of Education was small compared with those of the other states, and it had less experience in a number of areas. As a result, Pennsylvania was slower to implement many of the provisions of NCLB and provided less direct support to schools and districts. For example, Pennsylvania superintendents were less likely than their counterparts in California and Georgia to report receiving needed technical assistance from the state; fewer principals and teachers in Pennsylvania reported receiving information in a timely manner; and more teachers reported not understanding the state test results. National studies confirm that some state agencies have greater capacity challenges than others (CEP, 2007a, p. 2), and they document wide variation in the strategies states have employed to provide support services to schools and districts (U.S. Department of Education, 2007a, pp. 74–78). Our three-state study highlights some of the ways these capacity and support issues manifest themselves in particular states.

Georgia was unique among the three states in having science assessments in place in grades three through eight prior to NCLB. As a result, science assessments were more familiar to educators in Georgia, and more districts in the state were implementing progress testing in science. California had a distinctive policy with respect to test preparation during much of this period. The California Department of Education did not release any items from its state test, and it had a policy that discouraged test preparation behaviors that might appear to be inappropriate. As a result, teachers were less likely to report certain test-focused classroom practices.

Georgia Educators Were Relatively More Positive Toward NCLB Than Were California or Pennsylvania Educators

While there was general agreement among educators across the states on many of the issues we addressed, responses from Georgia were often more positive than responses from the other states. Furthermore, in some cases Georgia educators responded positively while educators in the other two states gave mixed or negative responses. These findings may be the result of better implementation: Georgia teachers were more likely to report that they received sufficient technical assistance than did teachers in other states. However, the Georgia advantage may also be due to "external" confounding factors. We hinted above at one possible explanation: Georgia educators were having more success meeting their AYP targets relative to educators in California and Pennsylvania because they had lower targets. Another possibility, which we did not explore in this study, is that Georgia educators are generally not affiliated with national unions; teacher unions in their desire to protect teachers' rights may resist external interventions like those associated with NCLB.

Looking Ahead

This study suggests that NCLB has led to distinctive accountability systems in each state, although each was derived from the same federal legislation. States used the flexibility in the law to develop accountability systems that reflect local conditions. The reauthorization of ESEA should recognize that this variation exists and develop policies accordingly. In some cases, new regulations may be needed to reduce or eliminate differences—e.g., to make proficiency in reading and mathematics similar across states. This study found a number of attitudes and behaviors associated with the overall level of student proficiency in the states. In other cases, it may be appropriate to relax rules to give states additional flexibility. This study suggests that school improvement efforts might be more effective if they were responsive to local conditions. Rather than imposing a fixed set of choices that apply when schools fail to achieve AYP for a given number of years, improvement efforts should be customized to address the specific causes of the failure and the capacity that exists locally.

There is also a lesson for SBA in general. Educators have become comfortable with the underlying SBA theory of action—set clear goals, develop measures, and establish consequences to encourage educators to achieve them. They are not comfortable when the implementation of that theory seems inconsistent with their local situation—e.g., when the standards do not match their local curriculum, when the proficient level seems unattainable for many of their students, or when their school is judged against targets that feel unattainable. It would seem that engaging educators in the development or refinement of the SBA framework (e.g., the reauthorization of NCLB) would be a good way to attempt to bridge this gap.

Sampling and Response Rate Tables

Tables A.1 through A.6 show the sampling and response rates for our study.

Table A.1
Size of K–12 Public School Systems, 2005–2006

Feature	California	Georgia	Pennsylvania
Districts	1,128	204	730
Schools	9,863	2,489	3,250
Teachers	309,198	108,535	122,397
Students	6,437,202	1,598,461	1,830,684

SOURCE: NCES (undated).

Table A.2
Student Demographic Characteristics, 2003–2004

Characteristic	California (%)	Georgia (%)	Pennsylvania (%)
White	30	48	75
Hispanic	47	8	6
Black	8	38	16
Asian	11	3	2
Eligible for free/reduced-price lunch	48	50	31
ELLs	24	5	3
Students with disabilities	11	12	15

SOURCES: ELL data for Pennsylvania come from Pennsylvania Department of Education (2006). All other data come from NCES (undated).

Table A.3
District Sample and Cooperation, 2003–2004, 2004–2005, and 2005–2006

Sampling	California	Georgia	Pennsylvania	Total
2003–2004				
Initial sample number	27	27	27	81
Replacement sample number	13	5	5	23
Total sample number	40	32	32	104
Number cooperating	19	25	24	68
Cooperation rate (%)	47.5	78.1	75	65.4
2004–2005 and 2005–2006				
Total sample number	56	37	39	132
Number cooperating	31	30	31	92
Cooperation rate (%)	55	81	80	70

Table A.4
School Sample and Cooperation, 2003–2004, 2004–2005, and 2005–2006

Sampling	California	Georgia	Pennsylvania	Total
2003–2004				
No. in sample	78	116	103	297
No. of cooperating schools	63	108	96	267
Cooperation rate (%)	80.7	93.1	93.2	89.9
2004–2005				
No. in sample	122	124	107	353
No. of cooperating schools	91	111	99	301
Cooperation rate (%)	75	90	93	85
2005–2006				
No. in sample	122	124	107	353
No. of cooperating schools	91	111	97	299
Cooperation rate (%)	74.6	89.5	90.7	84.7

Table A.5
Superintendent Survey Responses, 2003–2004, 2004–2005, and 2005–2006

Response	California	Georgia	Pennsylvania	Total
2003–2004				
No. of cooperating districts	19	25	24	68
No. completing superintendent survey	18	20	22	60
Survey response rate (%)	94.7	80	91.6	88.2
2004–2005				
No. of cooperating districts	31	30	31	92
No. completing superintendent survey	24	24	19	67
Survey response rate (%)	77.4	80.0	61.3	72.8
2005–2006				
No. of cooperating districts	31	30	31	92
No. completing superintendent survey	26	21	20	67
Survey response rate (%)	83.9	70.0	64.5	72.8

Table A.6
Principal and Teacher Survey Responses, 2003–2004, 2004–2005, and 2005–2006

Sampling and Response	California	Georgia	Pennsylvania	Total
2003–2004				
No. of cooperating schools	63	108	96	267
No. of principal survey responses	51	88	88	227
Principal response rate (%)	80.9	81.5	91.7	85.3
No. in teacher sample	692	1,522	1,073	3,287
No. of teacher survey responses	487	1,318	926	2,731
Teacher response rate (%)	70.4	86.6	86.3	83.1
2004–2005				
No. of cooperating schools	91	111	99	301
No. of principal survey responses	78	95	87	260
Principal response rate (%)	86	86	88	86
No. in teacher sample	1,013	1,605	1,050	3,668
No. of teacher survey responses	826	1,409	938	3,173
Teacher response rate (%)	81.5	87.8	89.3	86.5
2005–2006				
No. of cooperating schools	91	111	97	299
No. of principal survey responses	75	96	88	259
Principal response rate (%)	82.4	86.5	90.7	86.6
No. in teacher sample	972	1,574	1,059	3,605
No. of teacher survey responses	670	1,366	931	2,967
Teacher response rate (%)	68.9	86.8	87.9	82.3

Results Tables

For explanations of the abbreviations in the results tables, see the abbreviations list in the front matter.

Table B.1
Teachers Agreeing That Standards Are Useful for Planning Lessons

Standards	California, % (SE)			Georgia, % (SE)			Pennsylvania, % (SE)		
	2004	2005	2006	2004	2005	2006	2004	2005	2006
Math	91	88	90	91	88	86	76	73	81
	(2)	(2)	(2)	(1)	(1)	(2)	(3)	(3)	(2)
Science	86	84	81	90	84	83	44	43	54
	(3)	(2)	(3)	(1)	(2)	(2)	(4)	(3)	(3)

NOTES: Response options included strongly disagree, disagree, agree, and strongly agree. Percentages represent the sum of the agree and strongly agree responses.

Table B.2
Teachers Agreeing with Statements About Content Coverage of State Standards

Statement	California, % (SE)						Georgia, % (SE)						Pennsylvania, % (SE)					
	2004		2005		2006		2004		2005		2006		2004		2005		2006	
	Elem	Mid	Elem	Mid	Elem	Mid	Elem	Mid	Elem	Mid	Elem	Mid	Elem	Mid	Elem	Mid	Elem	Mid
State content standards for mathematics																		
Include more content than can be adequately covered in the school year	83 (3)	86 (3)	81 (3)	85 (3)	81 (3)	84 (4)	70 (3)	84 (2)	68 (3)	71 (3)	55 (3)	59 (4)	74 (4)	78 (6)	64 (4)	74 (6)	65 (4)	78 (5)
Do not cover some important content areas	15 (2)	23 (5)	20 (3)	21 (4)	24 (3)	27 (4)	22 (2)	27 (2)	21 (2)	24 (2)	17 (2)	27 (2)	15 (2)	30 (6)	22 (2)	34 (5)	23 (2)	34 (5)
State content standards for science																		
Include more content than can be adequately covered in the school year	60 (6)	74 (5)	65 (4)	79 (3)	60 (4)	79 (4)	56 (3)	82 (2)	53 (3)	78 (3)	43 (3)	56 (4)	49 (4)	78 (3)	55 (4)	62 (6)	60 (3)	77 (4)
Do not cover some important content areas	15 (4)	40 (7)	19 (3)	37 (4)	23 (3)	45 (7)	35 (3)	29 (3)	36 (2)	34 (4)	23 (2)	41 (3)	19 (4)	33 (6)	22 (4)	37 (9)	24 (3)	41 (5)

NOTES: Response options included strongly disagree, disagree, agree, and strongly agree. Percentages represent the sum of the agree and strongly agree responses.

Table B.3
Administrators Agreeing That State Assessment Scores Accurately Reflect Student Achievement

Respondent	California, % (SE)			Georgia, % (SE)			Pennsylvania, % (SE)		
	2004	2005	2006	2004	2005	2006	2004	2005	2006
District superintendents	95 (5)	65 (12)	68 (10)	78 (10)	68 (13)	84 (8)	32 (11)	49 (15)	44 (13)
Elementary school principals	65 (12)	34 (10)	60 (8)	78 (5)	75 (6)	70 (7)	58 (11)	56 (10)	64 (8)
Middle school principals	70 (13)	64 (11)	63 (13)	60 (8)	64 (8)	61 (8)	29 (11)	40 (12)	42 (11)

NOTES: Response options included strongly disagree, disagree, agree, and strongly agree. Percentages represent the sum of the agree and strongly agree responses.

Table B.4
Teachers Agreeing with Statements About State Math Assessments

Statement	California, % (SE)						Georgia, % (SE)						Pennsylvania, % (SE)					
	2004		2005		2006		2004		2005		2006		2004		2005		2006	
	Elem	Mid	Elem	Mid	Elem	Mid	Elem	Mid	Elem	Mid	Elem	Mid	Elem	Mid	Elem	Mid	Elem	Mid
The state math assessment																		
Is a good measure of students' mastery of content standards	38 (3)	39 (5)	42 (3)	38 (4)	42 (4)	47 (3)	56 (3)	55 (3)	60 (2)	57 (3)	59 (3)	57 (3)	38 (4)	36 (7)	45 (4)	50 (4)	50 (4)	42 (8)
Is too difficult for the majority of my students	48 (5)	70 (5)	47 (5)	65 (4)	46 (6)	54 (4)	26 (3)	48 (3)	31 (3)	46 (2)	25 (3)	36 (3)	59 (5)	75 (6)	47 (4)	64 (4)	40 (4)	61 (8)
Includes considerable content that is not in our curriculum	27 (5)	39 (6)	33 (3)	32 (4)	27 (3)	27 (2)	19 (2)	24 (2)	24 (2)	27 (2)	18 (2)	23 (3)	32 (4)	43 (5)	25 (3)	43 (6)	17 (3)	45 (5)
Omits considerable content that is in our curriculum	30 (5)	38 (4)	35 (3)	30 (3)	36 (4)	32 (3)	26 (3)	34 (3)	26 (2)	37 (3)	25 (2)	29 (3)	24 (3)	37 (4)	27 (3)	49 (5)	26 (3)	36 (3)

NOTES: Response options included strongly disagree, disagree, agree, and strongly agree. Percentages represent the sum of the agree and strongly agree responses.

Table B.5
Teachers Agreeing with Statements Regarding State Science Assessments

Statement	California, % (SE)						Georgia, % (SE)					
	2004		2005		2006		2004		2005		2006	
	Elem	Mid	Elem	Mid	Elem	Mid	Elem	Mid	Elem	Mid	Elem	Mid
The state science assessment												
Is a good measure of students' mastery of content standards	28 (7)	22 (16)	21 (8)	30 (10)	23 (5)	22 (10)	46 (4)	43 (4)	46 (3)	47 (4)	54 (3)	40 (3)
Is too difficult for the majority of my students	61 (8)	86 (9)	64 (7)	73 (18)	74 (5)	75 (15)	40 (3)	52 (4)	43 (3)	45 (3)	42 (4)	34 (3)
Includes considerable content that is not in our curriculum	37 (10)	52 (7)	44 (7)	54 (10)	52 (7)	78 (10)	32 (3)	33 (4)	33 (3)	39 (3)	29 (2)	31 (3)
Omits considerable content that is in our curriculum	26 (8)	18 (12)	36 (7)	28 (10)	39 (5)	24 (10)	29 (3)	43 (4)	28 (2)	45 (3)	25 (3)	40 (3)

NOTES: Pennsylvania is omitted from this table because that state did not have science assessments during these years. Response options included strongly disagree, disagree, agree, and strongly agree. Percentages represent the sum of the agree and strongly agree responses.

Table B.6
Elementary School Principals Reporting That State Test Results Are Available and Useful

	California, % (SE)						Georgia, % (SE)						Pennsylvania, % (SE)					
	2004		2005		2006		2004		2005		2006		2004		2005		2006	
Results	Avlb	Usfl	Avlb	Usfl	Avlb	Usfl	Avlb	Usfl	Avlb	Usfl	Avlb	Usfl	Avlb	Usfl	Avlb	Usfl	Avlb	Usfl
Reports of last year's test results for the students at your school *last* year	100 (NA)	87 (8)	98 (1)	81 (8)	100 (NA)	91 (5)	91 (4)	88 (5)	98 (2)	92 (4)	100 (NA)	100 (0)	96 (2)	79 (7)	96 (3)	84 (8)	100 (NA)	82 (7)
Reports of last year's test results for the students at your school *this* year	95 (3)	86 (9)	100 (NA)	86 (8)	96 (3)	93 (4)	100 (NA)	95 (4)	98 (2)	98 (2)	100 (NA)	100 (0)	96 (3)	81 (7)	99 (1)	93 (4)	100 (NA)	89 (5)
Test results summarized for each student subgroup	100 (NA)	70 (7)	100 (NA)	72 (9)	100 (NA)	95 (3)	100 (NA)	92 (4)	92 (4)	91 (4)	98 (2)	97 (2)	96 (3)	64 (8)	100 (NA)	59 (8)	98 (2)	74 (8)
Test results summarized by subtopic or skill	97 (2)	79 (9)	88 (8)	71 (10)	91 (5)	91 (6)	97 (3)	79 (4)	96 (3)	94 (3)	93 (4)	93 (4)	98 (2)	79 (8)	100 (NA)	85 (8)	99 (1)	93 (4)

NOTES: Response options included not available, available and not useful, available and minimally useful, available and moderately useful, and available and very useful. Percentages for useful represent the sum of moderately useful and very useful responses from principals who said that the test results were available.

Table B.7
Middle School Principals Reporting That State Test Results Are Available and Useful

Results	California, % (SE)						Georgia, % (SE)						Pennsylvania, % (SE)					
	2004		2005		2006		2004		2005		2006		2004		2005		2006	
	Avlb	Usfl	Avlb	Usfl	Avlb	Usfl	Avlb	Usfl	Avlb	Usfl	Avlb	Usfl	Avlb	Usfl	Avlb	Usfl	Avlb	Usfl
Reports of last year's test results for the students at your school *last* year	95 (5)	93 (6)	93 (7)	74 (11)	100 (NA)	78 (14)	97 (2)	75 (8)	98 (1)	89 (6)	100 (NA)	97 (3)	83 (14)	73 (14)	81 (16)	77 (16)	100 (NA)	78 (9)
Reports of last year's test results for the students at your school *this* year	98 (2)	98 (2)	100 (NA)	92 (4)	100 (NA)	89 (6)	88 (6)	75 (8)	100 (NA)	92 (5)	100 (NA)	100 (0)	87 (8)	65 (14)	100 (NA)	72 (16)	90 (7)	78 (10)
Test results summarized for each student subgroup	100 (NA)	96 (4)	100 (NA)	89 (7)	100 (NA)	92 (6)	98 (2)	84 (7)	96 (3)	89 (6)	100 (NA)	93 (5)	100 (NA)	56 (14)	100 (NA)	59 (14)	100 (NA)	78 (9)
Test results summarized by subtopic or skill	96 (3)	94 (4)	96 (3)	81 (8)	99 (1)	91 (6)	95 (3)	86 (7)	94 (4)	87 (6)	83 (10)	83 (10)	100 (NA)	81 (9)	100 (NA)	84 (9)	100 (NA)	87 (7)

NOTES: Response options included not available, available and not useful, available and minimally useful, available and moderately useful, and available and very useful. Percentages for useful represent the sum of moderately useful and very useful responses from principals who said that the test results were available.

Table B.8
Elementary School Teachers Reporting That Mathematics and Science State Test Results Are Available and Useful

Results	California, % (SE)						Georgia, % (SE)						Pennsylvania, % (SE)					
	2004		2005		2006		2004		2005		2006		2004		2005		2006	
	Avail	Useful	Avail	Useful	Avail	Useful	Avail	Useful	Avail	Useful	Avail	Useful	Avail	Useful	Avail	Useful	Avail	Useful
Math teachers																		
Mathematics test results summarized by student subgroup	83 (3)	29 (3)	86 (2)	36 (4)	90 (2)	39 (5)	56 (3)	8 (4)	88 (2)	51 (3)	89 (2)	53 (3)	71 (4)	29 (2)	81 (3)	27 (2)	81 (3)	29 (3)
Mathematics test results disaggregated by subtopic/skill	80 (4)	75 (4)	87 (2)	68 (3)	89 (2)	69 (4)	64 (3)	70 (3)	94 (1)	80 (2)	96 (1)	85 (2)	82 (3)	68 (3)	82 (3)	66 (3)	84 (3)	61 (3)
Science teachers																		
Science test results summarized by student subgroup	14 (2)	20 (13)	27 (4)	17 (5)	42 (4)	13 (4)	35 (4)	29 (6)	73 (3)	35 (3)	77 (2)	37 (3)	NA	NA	NA	NA	NA	NA
Science test results disaggregated by subtopic/skill	14 (2)	37 (14)	28 (5)	25 (8)	41 (3)	28 (5)	37 (4)	53 (4)	78 (3)	55 (3)	83 (2)	59 (3)	NA	NA	NA	NA	NA	NA

NOTES: Response options included not available, available and not useful, available and minimally useful, available and moderately useful, and available and very useful. Percentages for useful represent the sum of moderately useful and very useful responses from teachers who said that the test results were available. Georgia tested students in all grades in math and science. California and Pennsylvania did not test students in some grades, but percentages include all teachers who reported that the resource was available, regardless of grade level.

Table B.9

Middle School Teachers Reporting Availability and Usefulness of Mathematics and Science State Test Results

	California, % (SE)						Georgia, % (SE)						Pennsylvania, % (SE)					
	2004		2005		2006		2004		2005		2006		2004		2005		2006	
Results	Avlb	Usfl	Avlb	Usfl	Avlb	Usfl	Avlb	Usfl	Avlb	Usfl	Avlb	Usfl	Avlb	Usfl	Avlb	Usfl	Avlb	Usfl
Math teachers																		
Mathematics test results summarized by student subgroup	86 (4)	38 (5)	89 (3)	30 (5)	91 (3)	34 (5)	76 (2)	37 (4)	82 (3)	56 (4)	89 (2)	56 (3)	77 (4)	23 (4)	79 (5)	27 (4)	80 (4)	27 (6)
Mathematics test results disaggregated by subtopic/skill	85 (4)	71 (4)	82 (2)	59 (4)	88 (4)	63 (5)	85 (2)	74 (4)	90 (3)	83 (2)	92 (2)	83 (2)	81 (4)	71 (7)	75 (6)	65 (7)	81 (4)	59 (7)
Science teachers																		
Science test results summarized by student subgroup	15 (4)	23 (19)	20 (4)	21 (5)	21 (5)	16 (5)	53 (4)	41 (5)	77 (4)	51 (4)	80 (3)	47 (5)	NA	NA	NA	NA	NA	NA
Science test results disaggregated by subtopic/skill	15 (4)	47 (16)	18 (4)	43 (8)	20 (5)	31 (8)	57 (4)	57 (6)	82 (4)	70 (2)	87 (2)	67 (4)	NA	NA	NA	NA	NA	NA

NOTES: Response options included not available, available and not useful, available and minimally useful, available and moderately useful, and available and very useful. Percentages for useful represent the sum of moderately useful and very useful responses from teachers who said that the test results were available. Georgia tested students in all grades in math and science. California and Pennsylvania did not test students in some grades, but percentages include all teachers who reported that the resource was available, regardless of grade level.

Table B.10
Principals and Teachers Agreeing That They Receive State Test Results/Performance Information in a Timely Manner

Respondent	California, % (SE)			Georgia, % (SE)			Pennsylvania, % (SE)		
	2004	2005	2006	2004	2005	2006	2004	2005	2006
Elementary school principals	45 (4)	44 (8)	43 (7)	14 (3)	51 (5)	60 (9)	13 (4)	13 (6)	23 (12)
Middle school principals	35 (8)	23 (10)	22 (13)	9 (6)	39 (8)	59 (7)	17 (5)	34 (5)	19 (8)
Elementary school teachers	72 (10)	58 (5)	57 (4)	36 (9)	71 (3)	78 (4)	60 (8)	36 (5)	48 (5)
Middle school teachers	63 (5)	70 (3)	69 (4)	47 (3)	69 (3)	77 (3)	79 (3)	64 (3)	54 (4)

NOTES: Response options included strongly disagree, disagree, agree, and strongly agree. Percentages represent the sum of the agree and strongly agree responses.

Table B.11
Superintendents Reporting That State Assessment Data Are Useful for Decisionmaking

Action	California, % (SE)			Georgia, % (SE)			Pennsylvania, % (SE)		
	2004	2005	2006	2004	2005	2006	2004	2005	2006
Developing a district improvement plan	100 (0)	92 (4)	94 (6)	85 (9)	100 (0)	95 (5)	71 (11)	97 (2)	82 (11)
Focusing principal and/or teacher PD		96 (3)	94 (6)		100 (0)	85 (9)		91 (5)	89 (8)
Helping individual schools to develop school improvement plans	100 (0)	88 (7)	97 (3)	94 (6)	100 (0)	95 (5)	67 (8)	86 (9)	90 (8)
Making changes to the district's curriculum and instructional materials	100 (0)	89 (6)	99 (1)	89 (7)	90 (6)	90 (6)	97 (2)	92 (4)	88 (9)
Recommending specific instructional strategies		68 (11)	65 (10)		69 (13)	80 (10)		80 (10)	75 (11)
Making policies regarding how much time is spent on each academic subject	58 (14)	64 (11)	68 (10)	52 (14)	76 (10)	78 (10)	44 (12)	72 (12)	52 (14)
Allocating resources among schools		59 (11)	59 (11)		52 (14)	80 (10)		53 (15)	55 (13)

NOTES: Response options included not useful, minimally useful, moderately useful, and very useful. Percentages represent the sum of the moderately useful and very useful responses.

Table B.12
Principals Reporting That State Assessment Data Are Useful for Decisionmaking

	California, % (SE)						Georgia, % (SE)						Pennsylvania, % (SE)					
	2004		2005		2006		2004		2005		2006		2004		2005		2006	
Action	Elem	Mid	Elem	Mid	Elem	Mid	Elem	Mid	Elem	Mid	Elem	Mid	Elem	Mid	Elem	Mid	Elem	Mid
Developing a school improvement plan	84 (7)	86 (8)	79 (8)	77 (8)	98 (1)	87 (8)	97 (3)	95 (4)	100 (0)	94 (5)	94 (4)	100 (0)	75 (7)	86 (7)	70 (9)	88 (7)	70 (9)	95 (3)
Focusing teacher PD	75 (6)	65 (7)	73 (9)	72 (9)	86 (6)	65 (4)	71 (7)	80 (6)	86 (5)	83 (7)	88 (5)	87 (6)	75 (6)	53 (3)	78 (8)	71 (6)	65 (9)	83 (7)
Making changes to curriculum and instructional materials	76 (7)	87 (7)	69 (10)	90 (5)	94 (5)	85 (6)	85 (6)	81 (7)	78 (5)	83 (7)	85 (7)	84 (6)	69 (7)	71 (14)	82 (6)	89 (7)	70 (10)	86 (7)
Identifying students who need additional instructional support	77 (11)	94 (5)	73 (10)	85 (8)	81 (6)	92 (4)	94 (6)	97 (2)	96 (3)	94 (5)	97 (2)	100 (0)	60 (9)	64 (14)	63 (9)	65 (15)	70 (9)	75 (9)
Making decisions on how much time is spent on each subject	55 (14)	66 (10)	53 (12)	70 (11)	56 (11)	62 (10)	70 (9)	61 (9)	71 (8)	66 (10)	79 (8)	72 (9)	60 (11)	38 (11)	47 (9)	49 (14)	53 (9)	46 (12)
Identifying teacher strengths and weaknesses	25 (12)	39 (9)	47 (11)	63 (9)	69 (8)	43 (12)	70 (8)	52 (9)	78 (6)	60 (10)	76 (6)	73 (8)	32 (8)	28 (11)	39 (9)	36 (11)	33 (8)	20 (8)
Making decisions regarding student promotion or retention	44 (14)	58 (8)	45 (12)	57 (12)	60 (8)	73 (10)	76 (9)	65 (9)	79 (7)	76 (8)	90 (6)	88 (7)	25 (8)	23 (9)	22 (8)	36 (12)	27 (8)	24 (9)
Assigning students to teachers	36 (13)	30 (8)	7 (3)	47 (11)	23 (8)	54 (10)	47 (8)	53 (9)	57 (7)	62 (10)	62 (7)	65 (10)	12 (5)	9 (4)	10 (5)	26 (10)	10 (5)	30 (11)

NOTES: Response options included not useful, minimally useful, moderately useful, and very useful. Percentages represent the sum of the moderately useful and very useful responses.

Table B.13
Mathematics and Science Teachers Agreeing with Statements About the State Tests

Statement	California, % (SE)						Georgia, % (SE)						Pennsylvania, % (SE)					
	2004		2005		2006		2004		2005		2006		2004		2005		2006	
	Elem	Mid	Elem	Mid	Elem	Mid	Elem	Mid	Elem	Mid	Elem	Mid	Elem	Mid	Elem	Mid	Elem	Mid
Math teachers																		
State test results allowed me to identify areas where I need to strengthen my content knowledge or teaching skills	77 (3)	65 (4)	70 (4)	54 (4)	73 (3)	62 (5)	81 (3)	71 (3)	89 (1)	79 (2)	89 (2)	79 (2)	70 (4)	68 (7)	69 (4)	60 (5)	62 (4)	57 (5)
State test results helped me identify and correct gaps in curriculum and instruction	67 (4)	62 (5)	63 (4)	53 (4)	67 (3)	60 (6)	77 (3)	71 (3)	85 (2)	84 (2)	88 (2)	80 (3)	69 (3)	77 (6)	63 (3)	58 (4)	56 (4)	61 (4)
State test results helped me tailor instruction to individual student needs	52 (3)	35 (5)	54 (4)	35 (4)	59 (3)	42 (7)	70 (3)	65 (4)	84 (2)	78 (3)	85 (2)	79 (3)	28 (4)	56 (5)	40 (4)	50 (5)	36 (3)	42 (6)
Science teachers																		
State test results allowed me to identify areas where I need to strengthen my content knowledge or teaching skills	53 (13)	26 (18)	46 (8)	48 (11)	57 (8)	50 (24)	77 (4)	72 (4)	83 (2)	79 (2)	85 (2)	74 (3)	NA	NA	NA	NA	NA	NA

Table B.13—Continued

Statement	California, % (SE)						Georgia, % (SE)						Pennsylvania, % (SE)					
	2004		2005		2006		2004		2005		2006		2004		2005		2006	
	Elem	Mid	Elem	Mid	Elem	Mid	Elem	Mid	Elem	Mid	Elem	Mid	Elem	Mid	Elem	Mid	Elem	Mid
State test results helped me identify and correct gaps in curriculum and instruction	53 (13)	13 (9)	38 (7)	54 (12)	47 (6)	31 (12)	75 (3)	65 (4)	79 (2)	74 (3)	83 (2)	73 (3)	NA	NA	NA	NA	NA	NA
State test results helped me tailor instruction to individual student needs	24 (11)	13 (9)	30 (6)	41 (11)	42 (8)	8 (7)	65 (4)	52 (5)	72 (3)	58 (4)	74 (3)	64 (4)	NA	NA	NA	NA	NA	NA

NOTES: Teachers who said that they did not receive test results are excluded. Only teachers in grades in which state tests were administered in 2004–2005 are included. In Pennsylvania these grade levels were 3, 5, and 8. Response options included strongly disagree, disagree, agree, and strongly agree. Percentages represent the sum of the agree and strongly agree responses.

Table B.14
Districts Requiring Some or All Elementary and Middle Schools to Administer Progress Tests

School Type	California, % (SE)		Georgia, % (SE)		Pennsylvania, % (SE)	
	2005	2006	2005	2006	2005	2006
Math progress tests required at some or all						
Elementary schools	44 (13)	54 (12)	89 (6)	73 (11)	38 (14)	64 (14)
Middle schools	56 (14)	65 (12)	89 (6)	72 (11)	32 (13)	53 (14)
Science progress tests required at some or all						
Elementary schools	9 (4)	16 (8)	55 (14)	55 (13)	0 (NA)	6 (6)
Middle schools	17 (8)	27 (11)	43 (14)	65 (12)	0 (NA)	6 (6)

Table B.15
Teachers Required to Administer Mathematics and Science Progress Tests

Subject	California, % (SE)						Georgia, % (SE)						Pennsylvania, % (SE)					
	2004		2005		2006		2004		2005		2006		2004		2005		2006	
	Elem	Mid	Elem	Mid	Elem	Mid	Elem	Mid	Elem	Mid	Elem	Mid	Elem	Mid	Elem	Mid	Elem	Mid
Mathematics	56 (8)	31 (6)	62 (6)	42 (8)	67 (7)	51 (10)	73 (4)	55 (5)	77 (5)	62 (5)	81 (4)	63 (6)	30 (5)	28 (6)	47 (6)	50 (14)	56 (6)	60 (12)
Science	6	2 (1)	9 (3)	11 (4)	8 (4)	9 (4)	23 (5)	37 (5)	30 (6)	44 (6)	26 (6)	46 (7)	3 (1)	3 (1)	3 (1)	10 (4)	3 (1)	6 (2)

NOTE: Response options included yes and no.

Table B.16
Mathematics Teachers' Responses to Statements About Progress Tests

	California, % (SE)						Georgia, % (SE)						Pennsylvania, % (SE)					
	2004		2005		2006		2004		2005		2006		2004		2005		2006	
Statement	Elem	Mid	Elem	Mid	Elem	Mid	Elem	Mid	Elem	Mid	Elem	Mid	Elem	Mid	Elem	Mid	Elem	Mid
District or school requires you to administer a progress test[a]	56 (8)	31 (6)	62 (6)	42 (8)	67 (7)	51 (10)	73 (4)	55 (5)	77 (5)	62 (5)	81 (4)	63 (6)	30 (5)	28 (6)	47 (6)	50 (14)	56 (6)	60 (12)
Progress tests administered two to three times per year[b]	60 (9)	44 (7)	57 (7)	59 (9)	63 (8)	62 (12)	25 (5)	25 (4)	35 (6)	28 (5)	42 (6)	39 (6)	46 (8)	51 (9)	51 (6)	34 (4)	43 (5)	45 (11)
Progress tests administered approximately every six to eight weeks[b]	35 (9)	45 (9)	30 (7)	21 (7)	24 (7)	20 (8)	65 (5)	59 (5)	54 (6)	65 (5)	50 (5)	53 (7)	21 (5)	32 (9)	32 (4)	38 (4)	41 (5)	34 (7)
Progress tests administered approximately every two to four weeks[b]	5 (3)	10 (8)	13 (5)	20 (6)	13 (6)	17 (8)	11 (3)	16 (4)	10 (2)	7 (2)	8 (2)	8 (3)	33 (6)	17 (7)	17 (4)	28 (6)	17 (4)	21 (9)
Results are available the same or next day[c,d]	20 (6)	46 (13)	35 (6)	53 (8)	26 (6)	39 (6)	66 (5)	63 (6)	57 (6)	56 (6)	50 (6)	47 (5)	56 (6)	56 (11)	56 (6)	49 (11)	34 (5)	20 (12)
Results are available within one week[c,e]	38 (6)	37 (12)	30 (5)	24 (8)	9 (3)	5 (3)	20 (3)	22 (4)	25 (4)	24 (3)	9 (1)	21 (4)	21 (4)	20 (8)	24 (4)	28 (6)	7 (2)	7 (2)
There are consequences for teachers associated with performance on the tests[f]	5 (4)	1 (1)	3 (1)	6 (2)	4 (3)	6 (4)	5 (2)	13 (4)	9 (3)	7 (3)	8 (3)	7 (2)	6 (2)	4 (2)	4 (2)	7 (3)	3 (1)	3 (1)

[a] Response options included yes and no.
[b] Response options included two to three times per year, approximately every six to eight weeks, and approximately every two to four weeks.
[c] Response options included the same day administered, the next day, within one week, two to four weeks later, more than four weeks later, and the scores are not available to me.
[d] Percentages represent the sum of the same day and next day responses.
[e] Percentages represent within one week responses.
[f] Response options included yes, no, and don't know. Percentages represent yes responses.

Table B.17
Elementary School Teachers Agreeing with Statements About Tests

Statement	California, % (SE)			Georgia, % (SE)			Pennsylvania, % (SE)		
	2004	2005	2006	2004	2005	2006	2004	2005	2006
State test									
Mathematics tests are a good measure of students' mastery of state content standards	38 (3)	42 (3)	42 (4)	56 (3)	60 (2)	59 (3)	38 (4)	45 (4)	50 (4)
Mathematics test results help me identify and correct gaps in curriculum and instruction	67 (4)	63 (4)	67 (3)	77 (3)	85 (2)	88 (2)	69 (3)	63 (3)	56 (4)
Progress test									
Mathematics tests are a good measure of students' mastery of state content standards	48 (5)	57 (5)	62 (4)	73 (3)	62 (4)	69 (3)	74 (4)	70 (3)	70 (3)
Mathematics test results help me identify and correct gaps in curriculum and instruction	78 (5)	76 (5)	81 (4)	82 (3)	76 (3)	85 (2)	87 (3)	84 (3)	84 (3)

NOTES: The results displayed for "state test" include responses from teachers in grades in which state tests were administered in 2004–2005 and who reported having access to these results. For Pennsylvania, this included only teachers in grades 3 and 5. The results displayed for "progress test" include only teachers who reported being required to administer progress tests. Percentages represent the sum of the agree and strongly agree responses.

Table B.18
Middle School Teachers Agreeing with Statements About Tests

Statement	California, % (SE)			Georgia, % (SE)			Pennsylvania, % (SE)		
	2004	2005	2006	2004	2005	2006	2004	2005	2006
State test									
Mathematics tests are a good measure of students' mastery of state content standards	39 (5)	38 (4)	47 (3)	55 (3)	57 (3)	57 (3)	36 (7)	50 (4)	42 (8)
Mathematics test results help me identify and correct gaps in curriculum and instruction	62 (5)	53 (4)	60 (6)	71 (3)	84 (2)	80 (3)	77 (6)	58 (4)	61 (4)
Progress test									
Mathematics tests are a good measure of students' mastery of state content standards	48 (11)	59 (5)	69 (5)	68 (5)	68 (4)	69 (3)	39 (9)	69 (5)	64 (3)
Mathematics test results help me identify and correct gaps in curriculum and instruction	67 (9)	76 (5)	75 (3)	76 (5)	82 (3)	81 (3)	61 (7)	86 (4)	76 (5)

NOTES: The results displayed for "state test" include responses from teachers in grades in which state tests were administered in 2004–2005 and who reported having access to these results. For Pennsylvania, this included only teachers in grades 3 and 5. The results displayed for "progress test" include only teachers who reported being required to administer progress tests. Percentages represent the sum of the agree and strongly agree responses.

Table B.19
Superintendents, Principals, and Teachers Agreeing with Statements About Understanding AYP and the State Accountability System

Statement	California, % (SE)			Georgia, % (SE)			Pennsylvania, % (SE)		
	2004	2005	2006	2004	2005	2006	2004	2005	2006
I have a clear understanding of AYP criteria									
Superintendents	80 (14)			77 (12)			100 (0)		
Elementary school principals	78 (9)	92 (4)	99 (1)	97 (2)	100 (0)	96 (4)	95 (4)	96 (4)	93 (4)
Middle school principals	91 (5)	95 (4)	96 (3)	89 (5)	88 (6)	100 (0)	99 (1)	94 (6)	87 (8)
The district and/or state helps me to understand the state accountability system requirements									
Elementary school principals	85 (10)	81 (9)	93 (5)	84 (5)	86 (4)	91 (4)	83 (7)	84 (9)	96 (3)
Middle school principals	92 (6)	82 (8)	85 (6)	77 (8)	81 (6)	100 (0)	88 (6)	99 (1)	80 (5)
The state's accountability system is so complicated, it is hard for me to understand									
Elementary school teachers	54 (5)	52 (4)	42 (3)	50 (3)	39 (2)	36 (2)	56 (3)	45 (3)	43 (2)
Middle school teachers	56 (4)	55 (4)	58 (4)	46 (2)	44 (2)	42 (2)	54 (4)	48 (3)	41 (5)

NOTES: Response options included strongly disagree, disagree, agree, and strongly agree. Percentages represent the sum of the agree and strongly agree responses.

Table B.20
Superintendents and Principals Agreeing That District/School AYP Status Accurately Reflects Overall Student Performance

Respondent	California, % (SE)			Georgia, % (SE)			Pennsylvania, % (SE)		
	2004	2005	2006	2004	2005	2006	2004	2005	2006
Superintendents	48 (14)	60 (12)	41 (11)	14 (8)	44 (14)	40 (13)	27 (11)	30 (14)	51 (13)
Middle school principals	43 (11)	55 (12)	60 (9)	32 (7)	46 (8)	48 (9)	22 (9)	43 (13)	34 (11)
Elementary school principals	56 (14)	63 (10)	60 (11)	68 (6)	77 (6)	86 (6)	44 (11)	62 (10)	69 (8)

NOTES: Response options included strongly disagree, disagree, agree, and strongly agree. Percentages represent the sum of the agree and strongly agree responses.

Table B.21
Administrators Agreeing That District/School AYP Status Accurately Reflects Overall Student Performance, by District/School AYP Status

Respondent	California, % (SE)						Georgia, % (SE)						Pennsylvania, % (SE)					
	2004		2005		2006		2004		2005		2006		2004		2005		2006	
	Met AYP	Did Not Meet AYP	Met AYP	Did Not Meet AYP	Met AYP	Did Not Meet AYP	Met AYP	Did Not Meet AYP	Met AYP	Did Not Meet AYP	Met AYP	Did Not Meet AYP	Met AYP	Did Not Meet AYP	Met AYP	Did Not Meet AYP	Met AYP	Did Not Meet AYP
District superintendents	49 (17)	64 (26)	68 (12)	0 (NA)	47 (14)	29 (16)	28 (28)	6 (6)	93 (6)	12 (7)	66 (18)	20 (11)	37 (16)	17 (13)	47 (18)	0 (NA)	53 (14)	19 (18)
Principals	55 (12)	39 (6)	67 (12)	47 (16)	72 (9)	38 (10)	70 (6)	12 (5)	80 (5)	2 (2)	87 (4)	10 (5)	43 (11)	22 (13)	61 (8)	0 (NA)	66 (7)	11 (8)

NOTES: Response options included strongly disagree, disagree, agree, and strongly agree. Percentages represent the sum of the agree and strongly agree responses.

Table B.22
Administrators Agreeing That Their District/School Would Meet AYP Targets for the Next School Year

Respondent	California, % (SE)			Georgia, % (SE)			Pennsylvania, % (SE)		
	2004	2005	2006	2004	2005	2006	2004	2005	2006
District superintendents	85 (13)	88 (6)	76 (10)	50 (14)	69 (11)	89 (6)	74 (11)	58 (15)	79 (10)
Elementary school principals	89 (10)	72 (9)	91 (5)	97 (2)	100 (0)	93 (4)	89 (6)	93 (4)	95 (3)
Middle school principals	77 (11)	66 (10)	75 (9)	69 (9)	92 (4)	88 (6)	89 (6)	74 (17)	69 (14)

NOTES: Response options included strongly disagree, disagree, agree, and strongly agree. Percentages represent the sum of the agree and strongly agree responses.

Table B.23
Administrators Agreeing That Their District/School Would Meet AYP Targets in the Next Five School Years

Respondent	California, % (SE)			Georgia, % (SE)			Pennsylvania, % (SE)		
	2004	2005	2006	2004	2005	2006	2004	2005	2006
District superintendents	35 (13)	29 (12)	22 (9)	45 (13)	35 (13)	59 (13)	40 (13)	39 (15)	54 (14)
Elementary school principals	44 (13)	44 (11)	58 (11)	80 (6)	87 (6)	87 (6)	55 (10)	51 (10)	52 (7)
Middle school principals	56 (8)	44 (10)	33 (9)	65 (8)	71 (8)	60 (8)	43 (13)	49 (15)	47 (13)

NOTES: Response options included strongly disagree, disagree, agree, and strongly agree. Percentages represent the sum of the agree and strongly agree responses.

Table B.24
Principals Employing School Improvement Strategies

Strategy	California, % (SE)						Georgia, % (SE)						Pennsylvania, % (SE)					
	2004		2005		2006		2004		2005		2006		2004		2005		2006	
	Elem	Mid	Elem	Mid	Elem	Mid	Elem	Mid	Elem	Mid	Elem	Mid	Elem	Mid	Elem	Mid	Elem	Mid
Matching curriculum and instruction with standards and/or assessments	99 (1)	96 (4)	100 (0)	100 (0)	95 (5)	98 (2)	99 (1)	94 (4)	97 (3)	100 (0)	100 (0)	100 (0)	99 (1)	100 (0)	100 (0)	99 (1)	100 (0)	100 (0)
Using existing research to inform decisions about improvement strategies	98 (2)	92 (6)	100 (0)	94 (5)	95 (3)	85 (8)	96 (3)	95 (4)	100 (0)	99 (1)	100 (0)	99 (1)	93 (5)	100 (5)	94 (0)	94 (5)	88 (7)	90 (6)
Providing additional instruction to low-performing students			96 (3)	95 (3)	100 (0)	98 (2)			98 (2)	100 (0)	99 (1)	98 (2)			97 (2)	97 (3)	85 (7)	90 (6)
Increasing the use of student achievement data to inform instruction	99 (1)	100 (0)	93 (7)	100 (0)	90 (6)	98 (2)	100 (0)	96 (4)	100 (0)	94 (5)	100 (0)	98 (2)	99 (1)	95 (5)	91 (7)	100 (0)	100 (0)	92 (7)
Increasing the quantity of teacher PD	84 (8)	72 (8)	89 (5)	90 (6)	93 (4)	80 (10)	96 (2)	83 (6)	95 (3)	96 (3)	95 (3)	96 (4)	85 (7)	70 (14)	64 (9)	94 (4)	71 (9)	72 (10)
Improving the school planning process	87 (7)	96 (4)	74 (10)	85 (8)	94 (5)	83 (8)	100 (0)	94 (4)	100 (0)	84 (7)	100 (0)	94 (3)	77 (8)	100 (0)	81 (6)	99 (1)	73 (9)	72 (15)
Providing before- or after-school, weekend, or summer programs	82 (9)	81 (11)	84 (8)	92 (6)	97 (2)	62 (14)	90 (5)	97 (2)	86 (4)	86 (5)	93 (5)	95 (3)	65 (11)	70 (14)	77 (7)	59 (15)	69 (10)	63 (14)
Promoting programs to make the school a more attractive choice for parents	74 (10)	70 (9)	60 (9)	70 (10)	80 (9)	78 (9)	80 (6)	64 (10)	74 (6)	62 (9)	87 (6)	56 (11)	57 (8)	59 (12)	43 (8)	71 (11)	47 (10)	42 (12)

Table B.24—Continued

	California, % (SE)						Georgia, % (SE)						Pennsylvania, % (SE)					
	2004		2005		2006		2004		2005		2006		2004		2005		2006	
Strategy	Elem	Mid	Elem	Mid	Elem	Mid	Elem	Mid	Elem	Mid	Elem	Mid	Elem	Mid	Elem	Mid	Elem	Mid
Restructuring the day to teach content in greater depth (e.g., a literacy block)	63 (11)	53 (10)	62 (9)	36 (10)	75 (10)	43 (13)	67 (5)	49 (9)	79 (7)	53 (9)	79 (5)	59 (11)	54 (8)	31 (11)	61 (9)	43 (13)	73 (9)	38 (12)
Increasing instructional time (lengthening school day or year or shortening recess)			8 (5)	23 (8)	31 (7)	12 (7)			58 (7)	35 (8)	42 (8)	23 (7)			26 (9)	20 (8)	20 (5)	24 (9)

NOTES: Response options included not employed, employed and not useful, employed and minimally useful, employed and moderately useful, and employed and very useful. Percentages represent employed responses.

Table B.25
Elementary and Middle School Principals Identifying School Improvement Strategies as Most Important

Strategy	California % (SE)				Georgia % (SE)				Pennsylvania % (SE)			
	2005		2006		2005		2006		2005		2006	
	Elem	Mid	Elem	Mid	Elem	Mid	Elem	Mid	Elem	Mid	Elem	Mid
Matching curriculum and instruction with standards and/or assessments	58 (11)	57 (10)	53 (9)	47 (10)	62 (6)	46 (8)	55 (7)	65 (8)	63 (9)	59 (13)	51 (8)	59 (11)
Using existing research to inform decisions about improvement strategies	40 (11)	37 (11)	34 (10)	44 (9)	23 (5)	25 (8)	22 (6)	28 (10)	22 (6)	18 (8)	23 (6)	25 (10)
Providing additional instruction to low performing students	40 (11)	55 (11)	48 (15)	72 (9)	38 (6)	46 (10)	45 (9)	46 (8)	50 (9)	71 (10)	47 (9)	39 (10)
Increasing the use of student achievement data to inform instruction	71 (8)	44 (11)	53 (9)	21 (8)	68 (7)	66 (9)	57 (6)	61 (8)	52 (11)	34 (11)	59 (9)	59 (11)
Increasing the quantity of teacher professional development	36 (11)	25 (9)	31 (9)	35 (9)	23 (5)	21 (7)	42 (6)	30 (9)	25 (9)	19 (9)	18 (5)	31 (11)
Improving the school planning process	2 (1)	16 (7)	11 (7)	17 (9)	22 (8)	32 (8)	25 (7)	29 (7)	17 (8)	22 (10)	9 (3)	15 (8)
Providing before- or after-school, weekend, or summer programs	18 (6)	27 (10)	24 (9)	4 (3)	19 (6)	13 (6)	17 (6)	8 (3)	19 (5)	26 (10)	27 (8)	29 (11)
Promoting programs to make the school a more attractive choice for parents	0	21 (8)	11 (6)	13 (7)	3 (3)	14 (8)	4 (3)	5 (3)	2 (1)	19 (16)	7 (3)	12 (8)
Restructuring the day to teach content in greater depth (e.g., a literacy block)	13 (8)	8 (5)	17 (7)	16 (7)	24 (7)	20 (8)	22 (6)	25 (9)	26 (6)	18 (9)	24 (7)	16 (8)
Increase instructional time (lengthening school day or year or shortening recess)	2 (2)	2 (2)	5 (4)	1 (1)	17 (5)	5 (3)	1 (1)	1 (1)	3 (3)	1 (1)	1 (1)	13 (7)

NOTE: The question was identify up to three strategies that are most important for making your school better.

Table B.26
Principals Reporting Test Preparation Activities

| | California, % (SE) | | | | | | Georgia, % (SE) | | | | | | Pennsylvania, % (SE) | | | | | |
| | 2004 | | 2005 | | 2006 | | 2004 | | 2005 | | 2006 | | 2004 | | 2005 | | 2006 | |
Activity	Elem	Mid	Elem	Mid	Elem	Mid	Elem	Mid	Elem	Mid	Elem	Mid	Elem	Mid	Elem	Mid	Elem	Mid
Helping teachers identify content that is likely to appear on the state test so they can cover it adequately in their instruction	89 (7)	96 (4)	94 (3)	99 (1)	81 (9)	98 (2)	95 (3)	100 (0)	100 (0)	100 (0)	97 (3)	98 (2)	100 (0)	95 (5)	100 (0)	99 (1)	100 (0)	98 (2)
Discussing methods for preparing students for the state test at staff meetings	76 (8)	99 (1)	94 (4)	95 (4)	94 (5)	99 (1)	100 (0)	100 (0)	100 (0)	100 (0)	99 (1)	100 (0)	100 (0)	100 (0)	99 (1)	100 (0)	100 (0)	100 (0)
Distributing released copies of the state test or test items	49 (14)	31 (10)	60 (10)	61 (11)	85 (8)	67 (11)	96 (3)	78 (7)	88 (4)	98 (2)	88 (5)	100 (0)	98 (2)	90 (7)	96 (3)	96 (2)	96 (3)	91 (5)
Encouraging teachers to focus their efforts on students close to meeting the standards			85 (6)	93 (3)	71 (8)	70 (9)			90 (4)	93 (4)	91 (4)	99 (1)			77 (7)	57 (15)	73 (9)	64 (14)
Distributing commercial test preparation materials (e.g., practice tests)	41 (12)	36 (12)	59 (10)	61 (11)	57 (15)	54 (13)	87 (5)	73 (7)	90 (5)	88 (5)	89 (5)	94 (3)	75 (8)	89 (7)	93 (4)	88 (7)	79 (8)	92 (5)
Encouraging or requiring teachers to spend more time on tested subjects and less on other subjects	52 (11)	44 (8)	53 (11)	63 (9)	45 (7)	63 (13)	53 (8)	55 (9)	44 (7)	66 (8)	51 (8)	50 (11)	39 (9)	46 (13)	61 (11)	45 (13)	64 (8)	44 (12)
Discussing assessment anchors with teachers (PA only)	NA	NA	NA	NA	NA	NA	NA	NA	NA	NA	NA	NA			100 (0)	100 (0)	100 (0)	

NOTE: Response options included yes and no.

Table B.27
Districts Taking Certain Steps to Assist Schools with Aligning *Math* Curriculum and Instruction with Standards in the Past Three Years

Step	California, % (SE)		Georgia, % (SE)		Pennsylvania, % (SE)	
	2005	2006	2005	2006	2005	2006
Monitored or provided feedback on the implementation of state standards in classrooms	98 (2)	81 (9)	93 (4)	70 (12)	82 (10)	70 (13)
Mapped out the alignment of required textbooks and instructional programs to state *standards*	82 (11)	76 (10)	85 (6)	58 (13)	54 (15)	70 (12)
Mapped out the alignment of required textbooks and instructional programs to state *assessments*	68 (12)	51 (11)	87 (6)	68 (12)	49 (15)	62 (12)
Developed pacing plan or instructional calendar aligned with state standards	60 (12)	58 (11)	83 (8)	76 (11)	64 (15)	66 (14)
Established detailed curriculum guidelines aligned with state content standards	48 (11)	51 (11)	75 (13)	84 (11)	66 (15)	79 (11)
Provided sample lessons linked to state standards	65 (13)	88 (7)	70 (13)	71 (12)	76 (12)	67 (13)
Developed local content standards that augment state content standards	62 (12)	57 (11)	51 (14)	27 (13)	72 (15)	30 (14)

NOTES: Response options included mathematics; science; reading, language arts, and English; and none of these subjects. We asked respondents to select at least one option. Percentages represent mathematics responses.

Table B.28
Districts Taking Certain Steps to Assist Schools with Aligning *Science* Curriculum and Instruction with Standards in the Past Three Years

Step	California, % (SE)		Georgia, % (SE)		Pennsylvania, % (SE)	
	2005	2006	2005	2006	2005	2006
Monitored or provided feedback on the implementation of state standards in classrooms	43 (13)	54 (11)	92 (4)	69 (12)	40 (14)	39 (14)
Mapped out the alignment of required textbooks and instructional programs to state *standards*	54 (13)	51 (12)	76 (9)	60 (13)	34 (14)	58 (13)
Mapped out the alignment of required textbooks and instructional programs to state *assessments*	48 (12)	34 (11)	72 (10)	60 (13)	30 (13)	41 (13)
Developed pacing plan or instructional calendar aligned with state standards	24 (11)	24 (10)	72 (10)	67 (11)	32 (12)	29 (14)
Established detailed curriculum guidelines aligned with state content standards	27 (10)	27 (10)	70 (11)	70 (12)	48 (14)	63 (14)
Provided sample lessons linked to state standards	38 (12)	49 (12)	67 (13)	69 (12)	32 (12)	41 (14)
Developed local content standards that augment state content standards	35 (11)	31 (11)	47 (14)	50 (14)	49 (14)	69 (14)

NOTES: Response options included mathematics; science; reading, language arts, and English; and none of these subjects. We asked respondents to select at least one option. Percentages represent science responses.

Table B.29
Elementary School Teachers Reporting That District/State Actions to Align Math Curriculum/Instruction with Standards Were Useful

Action	California, % (SE)			Georgia, % (SE)			Pennsylvania, % (SE)		
	2004	2005	2006	2004	2005	2006	2004	2005	2006
Detailed curriculum guidelines aligned with state standards	80 (5)	83 (2)	82 (3)	85 (2)	89 (2)	91 (2)	83 (3)	87 (2)	87 (2)
A "pacing plan" or "instructional calendar"		70 (4)	77 (5)		83 (2)	89 (2)		84 (2)	82 (3)
Monitoring and feedback on implementation of state standards	57 (4)	56 (5)	51 (4)	69 (4)	63 (3)	72 (3)	61 (3)	58 (4)	64 (4)
Mapping out alignment of textbooks and instructional programs to state standards	72 (4)	74 (2)	69 (4)	85 (2)	77 (2)	80 (2)	78 (3)	83 (3)	81 (3)
Sample lesson aligned with state standards	62 (6)	65 (4)	63 (5)	82 (2)	75 (3)	76 (3)	78 (3)	72 (2)	77 (3)

NOTE: Percentages represent the sum of moderately useful and very useful responses from teachers who said that the action occurred.

Table B.30
Middle School Teachers Reporting That District/State Actions to Align Math Curriculum/Instruction with Standards Were Useful

Action	California, % (SE)			Georgia, % (SE)			Pennsylvania, % (SE)		
	2004	2005	2006	2004	2005	2006	2004	2005	2006
Detailed curriculum guidelines aligned with state standards	72 (7)	80 (4)	79 (3)	90 (2)	87 (2)	89 (2)	77 (4)	84 (3)	76 (5)
A "pacing plan" or "instructional calendar"		67 (7)	78 (7)		81 (3)	85 (2)		73 (8)	69 (6)
Monitoring and feedback on implementation of state standards	62 (7)	52 (6)	49 (6)	64 (3)	61 (3)	71 (2)	60 (4)	51 (5)	56 (4)
Mapping out alignment of textbooks and instructional programs to state standards	75 (6)	76 (5)	74 (5)	84 (2)	70 (3)	74 (3)	66 (9)	61 (8)	71 (4)
Sample lesson aligned with state standards	61 (9)	66 (6)	69 (6)	74 (3)	72 (3)	75 (3)	67 (6)	57 (7)	80 (5)

NOTES: Response options included did not occur, occurred and not useful, occurred and minimally useful, occurred and moderately useful, and occurred and very useful. Percentages represent the sum of moderately useful and very useful responses from teachers who said that the action occurred.

Table B.31
Principals Agreeing with Statements About District Support

Statement	California, % (SE)						Georgia, % (SE)						Pennsylvania, % (SE)					
	2004		2005		2006		2004		2005		2006		2004		2005		2006	
	Elem	Mid	Elem	Mid	Elem	Mid	Elem	Mid	Elem	Mid	Elem	Mid	Elem	Mid	Elem	Mid	Elem	Mid
When schools are having difficulty, the district provides assistance needed to help them improve	77 (10)	84 (9)	66 (11)	91 (6)	78 (11)	77 (9)	81 (6)	86 (3)	83 (6)	82 (4)	79 (6)	88 (4)	80 (7)	83 (6)	86 (8)	69 (16)	77 (8)	78 (9)
District staff provide appropriate support to enable principals to act as instructional leaders	61 (17)	69 (17)	61 (13)	82 (8)	63 (11)	66 (8)	74 (8)	81 (4)	80 (5)	77 (5)	75 (6)	79 (8)	75 (11)	65 (13)	66 (9)	58 (15)	64 (9)	57 (14)
District staff provide appropriate instructional support for teachers	76 (10)	67 (14)	68 (12)	74 (9)	69 (9)	72 (9)	78 (7)	80 (5)	84 (5)	75 (7)	87 (5)	76 (9)	79 (7)	61 (14)	74 (8)	90 (6)	77 (9)	67 (14)
District staff provide support for teaching grade-level standards to special education students (i.e., students in IEPs)			45 (11)	64 (10)	56 (14)	63 (10)			77 (6)	77 (8)	77 (7)	84 (6)			80 (5)	80 (9)	82 (6)	69 (15)
District staff provide support for teaching grade-level standards to ELLs (i.e., students with LEP)			62 (11)	74 (10)	61 (13)	70 (8)			74 (7)	76 (8)	81 (7)	76 (7)			84 (7)	91 (4)	85 (4)	70 (10)

NOTES: Response options included strongly disagree, disagree, agree, and strongly agree. Percentages represent the sum of the agree and strongly agree responses.

Table B.32
Districts Providing Technical Assistance to All Schools or Low-Performing Schools

	California, % (SE)						Georgia, % (SE)						Pennsylvania, % (SE)					
	2004		2005		2006		2004		2005		2006		2004		2005		2006	
Assistance	All	Low	All	Low	All	Low	All	Low	All	Low	All	Low	All	Low	All	Low	All	Low
Assisting the school in analyzing assessment data to identify and address problems in instruction	86 (8)	0 (NA)	89 (8)	3 (3)	88 (7)	5 (3)	98 (2)	2 (2)	100 (NA)	0 (NA)	99 (1)	1 (1)	81 (10)	3 (3)	97 (3)	3 (3)	91 (9)	0 (NA)
Assisting the school in implementing instructional strategies that have been proven effective	86 (8)	0 (0)	89 (9)	11 (9)	74 (10)	13 (2)	100 (NA)	0 (NA)	98 (2)	0 (NA)	96 (3)	4 (3)	78 (11)	0 (NA)	97 (3)	3 (3)	78 (12)	5 (5)
Assisting the school in analyzing and revising its budget to use resources more effectively	86 (8)	0 (NA)	65 (12)	16 (10)	67 (11)	6 (6)	53 (14)	0 (NA)	74 (10)	4 (3)	70 (13)	2 (2)	39 (12)	1 (1)	54 (15)	0 (NA)	34 (13)	1 (1)
Helping the school with school improvement planning	86 (8)	0 (NA)	87 (8)	2 (2)	81 (9)	6 (4)	85 (10)	15 (10)	95 (4)	5 (4)	97 (3)	3 (3)	59 (12)	7 (4)	63 (15)	19 (14)	59 (14)	7 (5)
Helping schools prepare complete and accurate data to comply with NCLB reporting requirements	85 (9)	0 (NA)	73 (12)	3 (3)	81 (9)	19 (9)	79 (12)	15 (11)	100 (NA)	0 (NA)	87 (11)	12 (1)	77 (11)	0 (NA)	71 (14)	15 (14)	66 (14)	34 (14)
Helping the school obtain additional PD based on scientifically based research	81 (9)	0 (0)	72 (12)	2 (2)	73 (10)	14 (4)	100 (NA)	0 (NA)	98 (2)	2 (2)	94 (5)	1 (1)	66 (12)	0 (NA)	98 (2)	1 (1)	81 (11)	9 (9)

Table B.32—Continued

Assistance	California, % (SE)						Georgia, % (SE)						Pennsylvania, % (SE)					
	2004		2005		2006		2004		2005		2006		2004		2005		2006	
	All	Low	All	Low	All	Low	All	Low	All	Low	All	Low	All	Low	All	Low	All	Low
Providing guidance for teaching grade-level standards to ELLs and/or special education students			79 (9)	8 (5)	75 (10)	2 (2)			90 (7)	8 (7)	93 (5)	3 (3)			78 (11)	0 (NA)	73 (13)	0 (NA)
Providing before- or after-school, weekend, or summer programs	44 (14)	23 (14)	57 (13)	18 (10)	71 (10)	7 (4)	82 (9)	12 (7)	86 (11)	2 (2)	80 (10)	16 (9)	62 (12)	10 (8)	39 (14)	24 (13)	74 (12)	0 (NA)
Providing additional instructional materials and books	80 (9)	2 (2)	57 (12)	17 (9)	68 (11)	7 (4)	44 (13)	30 (13)	80 (9)	18 (9)	75 (10)	20 (9)	72 (12)	0 (NA)	61 (15)	7 (4)	57 (14)	0 (NA)
Assisting the school in implementing parental involvement strategies	44 (14)	0 (NA)	57 (13)	10 (6)	59 (11)	4 (3)	74 (12)	18 (10)	94 (4)	4 (4)	55 (13)	27 (10)	44 (12)	6 (6)	41 (14)	33 (15)	38 (13)	14 (10)
Helping the school obtain more-experienced teachers	42 (13)	2 (2)	35 (13)	3 (2)	39 (11)	1 (1)	67 (13)	4 (3)	81 (12)	0 (NA)	71 (11)	4 (3)	33 (11)	0 (NA)	23 (14)	1 (1)	23 (10)	0 (NA)
Assigning additional full-time school-level staff to support teacher development	29 (11)	15 (13)	12 (7)	10 (5)	5 (5)	18 (8)	10 (6)	21 (9)	55 (14)	15 (7)	48 (13)	25 (10)	38 (12)	1 (1)	27 (12)	3 (2)	26 (11)	8 (8)
Providing a coach or mentor to assist the principal	15 (8)	0 (0)	19 (8)	21 (10)	15 (8)	17 (7)	34 (13)	26 (11)	41 (14)	40 (14)	42 (13)	14 (7)	12 (8)	4 (3)	11 (9)	9 (8)	5 (3)	0 (NA)

NOTE: Response options included no schools, low-performing schools, high-performing schools, and all schools.

Table B.33
Districts Requiring Some or All Elementary and Middle Schools to Offer Remedial Assistance to Students Outside the School Day

School	California, % (SE)		Georgia, % (SE)		Pennsylvania, % (SE)	
	2005	2006	2005	2006	2005	2006
Elementary	61 (13)	72 (11)	84 (12)	86 (7)	95 (4)	87 (9)
Middle	44 (12)	75 (11)	86 (11)	75 (12)	82 (11)	87 (9)

NOTES: Response options included none, some, and all schools. Percentages represent the sum of the some and all responses.

Table B.34
Districts Requiring Some or All Elementary and Middle Schools to Make Changes Targeting Low-Achieving Students

Change	California, % (SE)				Georgia, % (SE)				Pennsylvania, % (SE)			
	2005		2006		2005		2006		2005		2006	
	Elem	Mid	Elem	Mid	Elem	Mid	Elem	Mid	Elem	Mid	Elem	Mid
Creating *separate mathematics* classes for low-achieving students	39 (13)	56 (14)	23 (10)	34 (11)	57 (14)	56 (13)	34 (13)	43 (13)	54 (15)	51 (15)	19 (10)	27 (12)
Increasing the amount of *time spent on math* instruction specifically for low-achieving students	44 (13)	35 (13)	71 (11)	60 (12)	94 (4)	92 (4)	50 (13)	87 (7)	63 (15)	49 (15)	58 (14)	48 (14)
Eliminating some remedial math courses or instruction and requiring all students to take more challenging math courses or instruction	53 (14)	76 (10)	22 (9)	61 (11)	19 (9)	21 (9)	43 (14)	66 (13)	11 (5)	32 (12)	20 (11)	21 (11)
Increasing the amount of *time spent on science* instruction specifically for low-achieving students	6 (3)	12 (7)	4 (3)	2 (2)	30 (14)	33 (14)	34 (13)	34 (13)	0 (NA)	0 (NA)	2 (2)	2 (2)
Requiring all students to take *more-challenging science courses* or instruction	6 (4)	9 (5)	9 (9)	11 (11)	33 (14)	43 (14)	28 (28)	37 (37)	17 (14)	28 (15)	16 (16)	16 (16)
Creating separate science classes for low-achieving students	2 (2)	4 (3)	2 (2)	2 (2)	3 (2)	16 (11)	13 (11)	13 (11)	8 (7)	8 (7)	0 (NA)	0 (NA)

NOTES: Response options included none, some, and all schools. Percentages represent the sum of the some and all responses.

Table B.35
Principals and Superintendents Reporting New Curricula

Response	California, % (SE)						Georgia, % (SE)						Pennsylvania, % (SE)					
	2004		2005		2006		2004		2005		2006		2004		2005		2006	
	Elem	Mid	Elem	Mid	Elem	Mid	Elem	Mid	Elem	Mid	Elem	Mid	Elem	Mid	Elem	Mid	Elem	Mid
Principal reports implementing[a]																		
New math curriculum	70 (10)	55 (13)	10 (5)	29 (9)	26 (11)	52 (12)	39 (8)	44 (9)	20 (5)	22 (7)	22 (6)	52 (10)	30 (10)	49 (13)	29 (10)	38 (15)	39 (11)	31 (10)
New science curriculum	26 (11)	46 (13)	14 (7)	24 (12)	6 (4)	16 (8)	41 (8)	20 (8)	9 (4)	8 (6)	6 (3)	60 (9)	42 (12)	45 (13)	16 (8)	17 (8)	32 (9)	21 (8)
Superintendent reports requiring some or all schools to adopt[b]																		
New math curriculum	47 (14)	62 (14)	27 (12)	35 (13)	28 (11)	33 (7)	34 (12)	18 (9)	29 (11)	36 (13)	39 (13)	45 (12)	20 (10)	33 (12)	24 (12)	27 (12)	36 (14)	32 (14)
New science curriculum	33 (14)	36 (15)	13 (9)	26 (13)	16 (12)	15 (8)	7 (5)	7 (5)	14 (8)	18 (8)	23 (13)	33 (12)	29 (12)	29 (12)	23 (14)	23 (14)	47 (13)	30 (13)

[a] Response options included yes and no.

[b] Response options included none, some, and all schools. Percentages represent the sum of the some and all responses.

Table B.36
Principals of Schools Identified as Needing Improvement Reporting District or State Assistance

	California			Georgia			Pennsylvania		
Type of Assistance	2004 n=6	2005 n=17	2006 n=11	2004 n=24	2005 n=21	2006 n=21	2004 n=13	2005 n=8	2006 n=9
Additional PD or special access to PD resources	6	9	6	18	9	14	10	7	5
Special grants to support school improvement	5	7	3	12	10	14	8	7	7
A mentor or coach for you (e.g., a distinguished educator)	5	6	2	5	6	11	2	2	2
School support teams	2	3	3	9	8	10	4	4	4
Additional full-time school-level staff to support teacher development	4	2	3	11	4	7	4	3	1
Distinguished teachers	1	3	0	3	1	1	3	1	5

NOTE: Response options included yes and no.

Table B.37
Principals of Schools in Corrective Action or Restructuring Reporting District Interventions

	California		Georgia		Pennsylvania	
Intervention	2005 (n = 9)	2006 (n = 8)	2005 (n = 4)	2006 (n = 5)	2005 (n = 0)	2006 (n = 4)
Extending the school day or school year	2	2	3	0	NA	0
Appointing an outside expert to advise the school	0	4	2	2	NA	1
Reassigning or demoting the principal	0	0	2	1	NA	0
Significantly decreasing management authority at the school level	1	2	0	1	NA	1
Restructuring the internal organization of the school	1	2	0	0	NA	1
Replacing school staff who are relevant to the failure to make AYP	0	0	1	0	NA	1
Replacing all or most of the school staff	0	0	0	0	NA	0
Reopening the school as a public charter school	0	0	0	0	NA	0
Entering into a contract with a private management company to operate the school	0	0	0	0	NA	0

NOTE: Response options included yes and no.

Table B.38
Teachers Reporting Emphasis on PD Activities

	California, % (SE)						Georgia, % (SE)						Pennsylvania, % (SE)					
	2004		2005		2006		2004		2005		2006		2004		2005		2006	
Activity	Elem	Mid	Elem	Mid	Elem	Mid	Elem	Mid	Elem	Mid	Elem	Mid	Elem	Mid	Elem	Mid	Elem	Mid
Aligning curriculum and instruction with state and/or district content standards	65 (6)	61 (4)	68 (5)	52 (5)	63 (4)	60 (5)	67 (3)	64 (3)	79 (2)	68 (3)	83 (2)	75 (2)	63 (4)	61 (4)	70 (3)	64 (4)	60 (3)	59 (5)
Instructional strategies for low-achieving students	56 (3)	48 (5)	57 (5)	44 (5)	53 (4)	47 (5)	61 (4)	55 (3)	68 (3)	57 (2)	64 (3)	54 (3)	43 (3)	38 (2)	46 (3)	39 (5)	42 (2)	35 (3)
Preparing students to take the state assessments	31 (5)	31 (4)	47 (6)	28 (4)	42 (5)	31 (4)	65 (4)	56 (3)	74 (3)	56 (3)	69 (3)	62 (3)	66 (4)	57 (4)	67 (3)	58 (4)	62 (4)	55 (8)
Instructional strategies for ELLs	53 (5)	42 (5)	57 (5)	40 (5)	54 (5)	41 (6)	17 (2)	19 (3)	27 (2)	17 (2)	23 (2)	16 (2)	11 (2)	11 (3)	14 (2)	10 (3)	11 (1)	11 (2)
Math and math teaching	51 (6)	50 (5)	53 (4)	42 (5)	52 (5)	37 (5)	54 (4)	39 (3)	57 (4)	52 (3)	58 (4)	49 (2)	57 (6)	36 (4)	64 (4)	44 (3)	57 (4)	45 (4)
Interpreting and using reports of student test results	32 (5)	33 (4)	44 (6)	24 (3)	43 (7)	26 (3)	47 (4)	40 (3)	65 (3)	45 (4)	60 (4)	49 (3)	38 (4)	27 (3)	36 (4)	33 (7)	36 (4)	32 (5)
Instructional strategies for special education students	33 (4)	26 (4)	25 (4)	25 (4)	21 (3)	32 (3)	34 (2)	40 (3)	39 (2)	42 (3)	40 (3)	44 (3)	28 (3)	33 (3)	33 (3)	33 (4)	30 (2)	28 (4)
Science and science teaching	16 (3)	27 (4)	28 (4)	26 (4)	16 (4)	36 (6)	21 (3)	25 (2)	20 (2)	32 (2)	32 (3)	36 (2)	18 (2)	21 (2)	22 (3)	30 (5)	28 (4)	31 (6)

NOTES: Response options included no emphasis, minor emphasis, moderate emphasis, and major emphasis. Percentages represent the sum of the moderate and major emphasis responses.

Table B.39
Superintendents Reporting Need for Technical Assistance and Receipt of Assistance If Needed

Assistance	California, % (SE)				Georgia, % (SE)				Pennsylvania, % (SE)			
	2005		2006		2005		2006		2005		2006	
	N	R	N	R	N	R	N	R	N	R	N	R
Identify effective methods and instructional strategies in scientifically based research	79 (9)	53 (16)	16 (10)	64 (12)	70 (14)	74 (13)	71 (13)	93 (7)	88 (9)	38 (14)	14 (7)	55 (15)
Provide effective PD	74 (10)	69 (16)	69 (11)	61 (13)	72 (14)	92 (5)	69 (13)	93 (7)	77 (12)	58 (15)	78 (11)	53 (17)
Use data more effectively	48 (14)	57 (18)	72 (10)	73 (13)	74 (13)	90 (7)	80 (11)	100 (0)	87 (9)	55 (16)	85 (7)	63 (15)
Clarify accountability system rules and requirements	84 (8)	96 (4)	41 (11)	94 (6)	55 (15)	86 (13)	66 (13)	100 (0)	57 (15)	100 (0)	45 (14)	59 (21)
Develop and implement a district improvement plan	43 (13)	93 (6)	22 (10)	77 (10)	45 (15)	78 (16)	58 (13)	79 (15)	50 (15)	69 (24)	18 (10)	19 (15)
Develop curriculum guides or model lessons based on state content standards	34 (12)	31 (19)	47 (12)	56 (19)	50 (15)	90 (7)	58 (13)	100 (0)	86 (6)	62 (17)	65 (13)	41 (17)
Promote parent involvement	37 (12)	42 (20)	57 (11)	37 (16)	52 (14)	60 (18)	62 (13)	51 (17)	70 (13)	17 (14)	44 (14)	41 (22)
Help the district work with schools in need of improvement	37 (12)	78 (16)	39 (11)	55 (21)	62 (14)	100 (0)	60 (13)	89 (10)	39 (15)	30 (19)	33 (12)	36 (24)

NOTES: Response options included yes and no to whether needed, received, and sufficient. "N" is needed, and "R" is received, if needed.

Table B.40
Educators Reporting Changes in Their Schools or Districts as a Result of the State's Accountability System

| | California, % (SE) | | | | | | Georgia, % (SE) | | | | | | Pennsylvania, % (SE) | | | | | |
| | 2004 | | 2005 | | 2006 | | 2004 | | 2005 | | 2006 | | 2004 | | 2005 | | 2006 | |
Respondent	For Better	For Worse	For Better	For Worse	For Better	For Worse	For Better	For Worse	For Better	For Worse	For Better	For Worse	For Better	For Worse	For Better	For Worse	For Better	For Worse
Academic rigor of the curriculum																		
Super-intendents	65 (12)	4 (4)	61 (12)	2 (2)	62 (12)	0 (NA)	50 (14)	3 (3)	76 (10)	0 (NA)	57 (14)	1 (1)	62 (12)	7 (6)	61 (15)	9 (8)	57 (13)	12 (8)
Elementary school principals	39 (12)	19 (7)	61 (10)	10 (6)	81 (6)	0 (0)	57 (11)	0 (11)	62 (11)	0 (NA)	72 (8)	3 (3)	55 (11)	12 (6)	68 (8)	3 (2)	70 (8)	2 (2)
Middle school principals	50 (14)	4 (4)	79 (7)	2 (2)	52 (12)	2 (2)	54 (8)	0 (NA)	40 (11)	4 (4)	77 (7)	0 (NA)	49 (13)	3 (2)	38 (12)	2	45	1
Elementary school teachers	34 (5)	16 (3)	42 (4)	16 (3)	48 (7)	17 (3)	40 (3)	13 (2)	47 (3)	12 (1)	48 (3)	10 (2)	28 (3)	33 (3)	26 (3)	26 (3)	32 (3)	28 (3)
Middle school teachers	32 (5)	10 (3)	39 (4)	10 (2)	47 (5)	11 (3)	39 (3)	17 (2)	42 (3)	11 (1)	46 (3)	8 (1)	26 (3)	21 (2)	25 (3)	15 (2)	34 (4)	16 (3)
Principal/teacher focus on student learning[a]																		
Super-intendents	45 (14)	0 (NA)	68 (11)	0 (NA)			80 (10)	0 (NA)	84 (8)	0 (NA)			88 (7)	2 (2)	87 (8)	12 (8)		
Elementary school principals	57 (9)	15 (8)	81 (9)	0 (NA)	86 (5)	0	0 (7)	3 (3)	77 (6)	2 (2)	79 (8)	0 (NA)	61 (9)	11 (5)	73 (8)	4 (3)	75 (8)	6 (4)
Middle school principals	63 (18)	0 (NA)	79 (10)	5 (4)	74 (10)	0 (NA)	69 (8)	0 (NA)	80 (7)	0 (NA)	93 (3)	0 (NA)	70 (10)	5 (3)	45 (13)	7 (4)	70 (10)	3 (2)
Elementary school teachers	44 (6)	9 (2)	44 (5)	12 (3)	53 (7)	10 (2)	2 (3)	6 (1)	59 (3)	3 (1)	62 (3)	5 (1)	39 (4)	15 (3)	45 (3)	8 (2)	40 (4)	10 (2)
Middle school teachers	36 (5)	8 (2)	48 (5)	6 (2)	50 (4)	6 (2)	52 (3)	10 (1)	63 (3)	7 (2)	59 (3)	4 (1)	35 (4)	19 (3)	36 (7)	12 (2)	39 (4)	8 (2)

Table B.40—Continued

	California, % (SE)						Georgia, % (SE)						Pennsylvania, % (SE)					
	2004		2005		2006		2004		2005		2006		2004		2005		2006	
Respondent	For Better	For Worse	For Better	For Worse	For Better	For Worse	For Better	For Worse	For Better	For Worse	For Better	For Worse	For Better	For Worse	For Better	For Worse	For Better	For Worse
Students' focus on school work[b]																		
Elementary school principals	36 (12)	11 (7)	30 (10)	0 (NA)	46 (9)	0 (NA)	48 (7)	0 (NA)	51 (8)	0 (NA)	59 (8)	0 (NA)	30 (10)	1 (1)	21 (6)	7 (4)	37 (7)	6 (4)
Middle school principals	21 (12)	4 (4)	51 (11)	2 (2)	43 (13)	0 (NA)	42 (9)	0 (NA)	42 (10)	0 (NA)	40 (9)	0 (NA)	18 (7)	1 (1)	27 (11)	3 (2)	24 (9)	4 (3)
Elementary school teachers	22 (5)	5 (2)	23 (4)	9 (2)	31 (5)	5 (2)	27 (3)	6 (1)	36 (3)	5 (1)	34 (3)	6 (2)	13 (2)	12 (2)	15 (2)	10 (2)	20 (3)	11 (2)
Middle school teachers	13 (3)	9 (2)	20 (2)	10 (2)	21 (5)	9 (2)	18 (2)	13 (2)	21 (2)	16 (3)	28 (3)	10 (1)	10 (2)	14 (4)	10 (3)	10 (2)	13 (4)	14 (3)
Students' learning of important skills and knowledge[b]																		
Elementary school principals	43 (12)	11 (7)	60 (9)	1 (1)	66 (7)	0 (0)	59 (7)	0 (NA)	72 (7)	0 (NA)	75 (7)	0 (NA)	45 (11)	8 (6)	57 (8)	7 (5)	56 (9)	10 (5)
Middle school principals	42 (17)	0 (NA)	66 (11)	2 (2)	50 (12)	8 (8)	55 (8)	1 (1)	56 (10)	0 (NA)	75 (8)	2 (2)	36 (12)	0 (NA)	33 (12)	23 (17)	73 (9)	1 (1)
Elementary school teachers	31 (5)	6 (1)	35 (4)	8 (2)	46 (6)	8 (2)	41 (3)	6 (1)	49 (3)	4 (1)	47 (3)	5 (1)	23 (3)	12 (2)	30 (3)	8 (2)	32 (3)	11 (2)
Middle school teachers	30 (4)	11 (3)	36 (3)	10 (2)	39 (4)	9 (2)	36 (3)	10 (1)	37 (2)	8 (2)	42 (2)	7 (1)	17 (4)	16 (3)	25 (7)	12 (5)	25 (5)	15 (2)

NOTE: Response options included changed for the worse, did not change due to accountability system, and changed for the better.

[a] We asked superintendents about principals' focus on student learning. We asked principals about teachers' focus.

[b] We did not ask superintendents this question.

Table B.41
Teachers and Principals Agreeing That the State's Accountability System Has Been Beneficial for Students

Respondent	California, % (SE)			Georgia, % (SE)			Pennsylvania, % (SE)		
	2004	2005	2006	2004	2005	2006	2004	2005	2006
Elementary school principals		51 (13)	79 (8)		77 (6)	88 (5)		67 (9)	71 (8)
Middle school principals		77 (7)	70 (8)		60 (9)	76 (8)		56 (14)	61 (12)
Elementary school teachers	40 (5)	28 (3)	37 (5)	45 (2)	54 (2)	54 (3)	22 (4)	30 (3)	31 (4)
Middle school teachers	32 (5)	34 (3)	34 (5)	44 (2)	50 (2)	50 (2)	29 (4)	29 (3)	28 (3)

NOTES: Response options included strongly disagree, disagree, agree, and strongly agree. Percentages represent the sum of the agree and strongly agree responses.

Table B.42
Teachers Indicating Various Changes in Their Schools as a Result of the State's Accountability System

Respondent	California, % (SE)						Georgia, % (SE)						Pennsylvania, % (SE)					
	2004		2005		2006		2004		2005		2006		2004		2005		2006	
	For Better	For Worse	For Better	For Worse	For Better	For Worse	For Better	For Worse	For Better	For Worse	For Better	For Worse	For Better	For Worse	For Better	For Worse	For Better	For Worse
The principal's effectiveness as an instructional leader																		
Elementary school teachers	25 (7)	7 (2)	31 (5)	11 (3)	38 (6)	9 (2)	41 (4)	7 (1)	46 (3)	8 (2)	41 (3)	8 (2)	26 (3)	10 (2)	27 (2)	9 (2)	24 (3)	10 (3)
Middle school teachers	31 (5)	9 (3)	30 (3)	8 (2)	28 (4)	14 (4)	32 (2)	13 (2)	44 (3)	13 (2)	37 (3)	12 (1)	25 (2)	14 (3)	21 (3)	19 (7)	24 (5)	10 (2)
Teachers' relationships with their students																		
Elementary school teachers	14 (4)	12 (2)	22 (4)	14 (3)	27 (5)	16 (3)	30 (3)	9 (2)	34 (3)	5 (1)	34 (3)	7 (1)	14 (2)	17 (2)	16 (2)	11 (2)	18 (2)	15 (2)
Middle school teachers	10 (2)	10 (2)	18 (3)	11 (2)	19 (2)	10 (2)	26 (2)	11 (2)	33 (3)	10 (2)	31 (2)	9 (2)	9 (2)	10 (4)	14 (2)	6 (2)	13 (3)	10 (2)
My own teaching practice																		
Elementary school teachers	33 (5)	8 (2)	43 (5)	10 (2)	51 (6)	8 (1)	51 (4)	5 (1)	59 (4)	5 (1)	61 (4)	5 (1)	38 (4)	15 (3)	40 (3)	11 (2)	43 (4)	12 (2)
Middle school teachers	37 (5)	8 (2)	45 (4)	6 (2)	48 (5)	6 (2)	52 (3)	7 (1)	56 (3)	4 (1)	56 (3)	3 (1)	37 (3)	11 (3)	32 (5)	4 (1)	44 (4)	6 (2)

NOTE: Response options included changed for the worse, did not change due to accountability system, and changed for the better.

Table B.43
Elementary School Teachers Reporting That Their Instruction Differs as a Result of Mathematics and Science Assessments

Difference	California, % (SE)						Georgia, % (SE)						Pennsylvania, % (SE)[a]					
	2004		2005		2006		2004		2005		2006		2004		2005		2006	
	Math	Sci	Math	Sci	Math	Sci	Math	Sci	Math	Sci	Math	Sci	Math	Sci	Math	Sci	Math	Sci
Assign more homework	37 (4)	8 (2)	42 (4)	8 (2)	31 (4)	11 (2)	33 (4)	18 (3)	29 (4)	21 (3)	32 (3)	20 (3)	31 (4)	NA	30 (4)	NA	30 (3)	NA
Spend more time teaching content	53 (5)	27 (4)	52 (3)	29 (4)	51 (5)	26 (3)	58 (3)	43 (4)	58 (4)	43 (4)	58 (3)	46 (4)	55 (4)	NA	53 (4)	NA	55 (4)	NA
Offer more assistance outside of school for students who are not proficient	26 (5)	4 (2)	29 (3)	8 (2)	27 (4)	10 (3)	31 (4)	15 (3)	34 (3)	16 (3)	33 (4)	15 (2)	14 (2)	NA	21 (3)	NA	21 (3)	NA
Search for more effective teaching methods	76 (3)	44 (4)	67 (3)	33 (4)	62 (5)	39 (4)	77 (3)	73 (4)	74 (4)	64 (5)	76 (3)	67 (3)	76 (3)	NA	60 (4)	NA	60 (3)	NA
Focus more on standards	84 (3)	47 (6)	73 (4)	45 (4)	68 (5)	48 (3)	85 (2)	85 (3)	77 (3)	68 (4)	76 (3)	72 (4)	74 (3)	NA	76 (3)	NA	78 (3)	NA
Focus more on topics emphasized in assessment	62 (3)	21 (5)	63 (5)	35 (4)	64 (4)	28 (3)	70 (4)	60 (4)	72 (3)	57 (4)	71 (4)	62 (5)	75 (3)	NA	72 (3)	NA	71 (4)	NA
Emphasize assessment styles and formats of problems	46 (4)	16 (3)	55 (4)	20 (4)	56 (5)	23 (3)	72 (3)	65 (4)	78 (3)	59 (4)	75 (3)	63 (4)	77 (3)	NA	74 (3)	NA	81 (3)	NA
Spend more time teaching test-taking strategies	53 (5)	15 (4)	53 (4)	25 (4)	53 (5)	27 (3)	56 (3)	45 (3)	56 (4)	42 (4)	59 (3)	47 (5)	57 (3)	NA	51 (3)	NA	56 (3)	NA
Focus more on students who are close to proficient	27 (4)	11 (3)	37 (4)	9 (2)	41 (4)	14 (2)	28 (4)	17 (3)	36 (2)	23 (3)	39 (3)	31 (3)	28 (3)	NA	29 (2)	NA	30 (3)	NA

Table B.43—Continued

Difference	California, % (SE)						Georgia, % (SE)						Pennsylvania, % (SE)[a]					
	2004		2005		2006		2004		2005		2006		2004		2005		2006	
	Math	Sci	Math	Sci	Math	Sci	Math	Sci	Math	Sci	Math	Sci	Math	Sci	Math	Sci	Math	Sci
Rely more heavily on multiple-choice tests	22 (3)	16 (4)	24 (5)	19 (4)	29 (5)	23 (3)	38 (4)	41 (4)	37 (4)	41 (4)	37 (3)	40 (4)	19 (3)	NA	18 (3)	NA	23 (2)	NA
Rely more heavily on open-ended tests	33 (5)	25 (3)	21 (4)	17 (3)	21 (3)	19 (3)	26 (4)	34 (5)	23 (4)	27 (3)	27 (2)	30 (3)	61 (4)	NA	50 (2)	NA	46 (3)	NA

NOTES: Response options included not at all, a small amount, a moderate amount, and a great deal. Percentages represent the sum of a moderate amount and a great deal responses.

[a] We did not present these questions to Pennsylvania science teachers because there was no state science test.

Table B.44
Middle School Teachers Reporting That Their Instruction Differs as a Result of Mathematics and Science Assessments

| | California, % (SE) | | | | | | Georgia, % (SE) | | | | | | Pennsylvania, % (SE) | | | | | |
| | 2004 | | 2005 | | 2006 | | 2004 | | 2005 | | 2006 | | 2004 | | 2005 | | 2006 | |
Difference	Math	Sci	Math	Sci	Math	Sci	Math	Sci	Math	Sci	Math	Sci	Math	Sci	Math	Sci	Math	Sci
Assign more homework	38 (7)	15 (4)	29 (4)	8 (3)	21 (4)	11 (3)	31 (3)	25 (3)	29 (3)	26 (3)	23 (2)	23 (2)	19 (3)	NA	13 (3)	NA	28 (4)	NA
Spend more time teaching content	67 (5)	50 (5)	58 (3)	35 (6)	57 (5)	41 (5)	73 (3)	76 (3)	69 (3)	67 (3)	69 (3)	71 (3)	64 (3)	NA	59 (7)	NA	59 (6)	NA
Offer more assistance outside of school for students who are not proficient	77 (4)	62 (5)	66 (4)	46 (6)	69 (5)	53 (7)	80 (3)	83 (3)	72 (3)	77 (3)	72 (3)	81 (3)	66 (5)	NA	69 (3)	NA	74 (4)	NA
Search for more effective teaching methods	75 (4)	28 (7)	57 (5)	27 (7)	56 (5)	41 (7)	71 (3)	62 (4)	73 (3)	64 (4)	72 (2)	63 (3)	56 (5)	NA	71 (7)	NA	75 (5)	NA
Focus more on standards	49 (6)	18 (5)	44 (5)	23 (4)	52 (6)	23 (6)	67 (4)	66 (3)	71 (3)	65 (3)	69 (3)	65 (4)	57 (6)	NA	62 (4)	NA	72 (5)	NA
Focus more on topics emphasized in assessment	50 (6)	27 (8)	45 (7)	26 (6)	45 (6)	24 (7)	44 (4)	44 (3)	44 (3)	48 (3)	48 (3)	44 (3)	39 (6)	NA	38 (4)	NA	41 (4)	NA
Emphasize assessment styles and formats of problems	64 (5)	44 (5)	45 (6)	24 (4)	40 (4)	25 (3)	64 (3)	63 (3)	53 (3)	59 (4)	53 (2)	49 (4)	44 (4)	NA	46 (3)	NA	49 (5)	NA
Spend more time teaching test-taking strategies	33 (7)	16 (6)	19 (3)	8 (2)	22 (3)	12 (3)	26 (3)	24 (3)	37 (4)	30 (3)	39 (4)	30 (4)	16 (3)	NA	22 (5)	NA	31 (3)	NA
Focus more on students who are close to proficient	38 (7)	15 (5)	26 (3)	9 (2)	30 (4)	8 (2)	44 (4)	29 (4)	41 (3)	33 (3)	44 (4)	27 (2)	26 (5)	NA	19 (5)	NA	22 (4)	NA

Table B.44—Continued

Difference	California, % (SE)						Georgia, % (SE)						Pennsylvania, % (SE)					
	2004		2005		2006		2004		2005		2006		2004		2005		2006	
	Math	Sci	Math	Sci	Math	Sci	Math	Sci	Math	Sci	Math	Sci	Math	Sci	Math	Sci	Math	Sci
Rely more heavily on multiple-choice tests	25 (6)	15 (5)	23 (3)	20 (3)	19 (6)	24 (4)	35 (5)	59 (4)	38 (4)	54 (3)	35 (5)	47 (3)	19 (4)	NA	9 (2)	NA	17 (4)	NA
Rely more heavily on open-ended tests	29 (3)	30 (6)	12 (2)	11 (2)	17 (5)	11 (3)	30 (3)	33 (3)	23 (2)	26 (3)	20 (3)	27 (3)	39 (4)	NA	33 (5)	NA	46 (6)	NA

NOTES: Response options included not at all, a small amount, a moderate amount, and a great deal. Percentages represent the sum of a moderate amount and a great deal responses.

[a] We did not present these questions to Pennsylvania science teachers because there was no state science test.

Table B.45
Administrators Reporting Various Changes as a Result of the State's Accountability System

	California, % (SE)						Georgia, % (SE)						Pennsylvania, % (SE)					
	2004		2005		2006		2004		2005		2006		2004		2005		2006	
Respondent	For Better	For Worse	For Better	For Worse	For Better	For Worse	For Better	For Worse	For Better	For Worse	For Better	For Worse	For Better	For Worse	For Better	For Worse	For Better	For Worse
Coordination of mathematics curriculum across grades																		
Super-intendents	41 (14)	4 (4)	73 (10)	0 (NA)	63 (11)	0 (NA)	29 (13)	3 (3)	49 (14)	2 (2)	63 (14)	0 (NA)	72 (11)	6 (6)	76 (14)	2 (2)	99 (1)	0 (NA)
Elementary school principals	48 (11)	0 (NA)	50 (12)	0 (NA)	37 (8)	0 (0)	37 (8)	0 (NA)	51 (8)	0 (NA)	52 (9)	0 (NA)	67 (11)	0 (NA)	76 (8)	1 (1)	63 (9)	0 (NA)
Middle school principals	47 (10)	0 (NA)	67 (10)	0 (NA)	78 (9)	0 (NA)	55 (9)	0 (NA)	46 (9)	0 (NA)	64 (9)	4 (4)	76 (9)	0 (NA)	82 (8)	0 (NA)	71 (8)	2 (2)
Coordination of science curriculum across grade levels																		
Super-intendents	20 (10)	23 (13)	54 (12)	1 (1)	13 (7)	0 (NA)	8 (5)	3 (3)	43 (14)	4 (3)	58 (14)	0 (NA)	35 (12)	2 (3)	42 (15)	2 (2)	58 (13)	0 (NA)
Elementary school principals	28 (12)	0 (NA)	27 (10)	0 (NA)	21 (5)	0 (NA)	29 (9)	0 (NA)	33 (9)	0 (NA)	37 (9)	0 (NA)	40 (10)	4 (3)	30 (10)	9 (7)	36 (10)	8 (6)
Middle school principals	22 (10)	0 (NA)	45 (10)	0 (NA)	43 (13)	0 (NA)	30 (7)	0 (NA)	20 (5)	0 (NA)	69 (8)	2 (2)	52 (12)	2 (1)	45 (14)	0 (NA)	47 (11)	0 (NA)
Extent to which innovative curricular programs or instructional approaches are used																		
Elementary school principals			32 (10)	19 (9)	43 (12)	21 (7)			64 (6)	0 (NA)	65 (7)	0 (NA)			42 (9)	9 (5)	47 (8)	8 (6)
Middle school principals			26 (7)	20 (10)	38 (13)	22 (11)			37 (9)	2 (2)	45 (10)	6 (6)			38 (12)	4 (3)	45 (11)	3 (2)

NOTE: Response options included changed for the worse, did not change due to accountability system, and changed for the better.

Table B.46
Educators Reporting Changes in Staff Morale as a Result of the State's Accountability System

Respondent	California, % (SE)			Georgia, % (SE)			Pennsylvania, % (SE)		
	2004	2005	2006	2004	2005	2006	2004	2005	2006
Change for the better									
District superintendents	0 (NA)	0 (NA)	0 (NA)	6 (4)	12 (11)	35 (14)	0 (NA)	10 (9)	16 (11)
Elementary school principals	3 (2)	5 (4)	15 (10)	20 (6)	20 (5)	23 (8)	7 (5)	8 (5)	9 (4)
Middle school principals	16 (12)	22 (8)	4 (3)	28 (8)	19 (7)	23 (10)	18 (9)	13 (8)	13 (8)
Elementary school teachers	7 (3)	10 (3)	17 (3)	15 (2)	20 (2)	17 (2)	6 (1)	6 (1)	9 (2)
Middle school teachers	8 (3)	10 (2)	11 (3)	13 (2)	15 (2)	20 (3)	5 (2)	4 (1)	4 (1)
Change for the worse									
District superintendents	69 (12)	77 (11)	77 (10)	51 (14)	76 (13)	38 (12)	72 (11)	77 (12)	55 (13)
Elementary school principals	63 (8)	65 (11)	43 (8)	38 (9)	27 (5)	36 (9)	53 (10)	53 (10)	44 (7)
Middle school principals	37 (8)	34 (10)	19 (9)	35 (8)	41 (8)	33 (10)	67 (12)	53 (13)	35 (10)
Elementary school teachers	56 (4)	48 (4)	46 (4)	47 (2)	39 (4)	39 (3)	73 (4)	63 (4)	60 (5)
Middle school teachers	59 (4)	49 (4)	48 (4)	56 (3)	50 (3)	45 (3)	72 (3)	66 (3)	63 (4)

NOTES: Response options included strongly disagree, disagree, agree, and strongly agree. Percentages represent the sum of the agree and strongly agree responses.

Table B.47
Teachers in Tested Grades Reporting Aligning Their Instruction with State Assessments and State Content Standards

Measure	California, % (SE)						Georgia, % (SE)						Pennsylvania, % (SE)					
	2004		2005		2006		2004		2005		2006		2004		2005		2006	
	Elem	Mid	Elem	Mid	Elem	Mid	Elem	Mid	Elem	Mid	Elem	Mid	Elem	Mid	Elem	Mid	Elem	Mid
Math teachers																		
Standards	97 (1)	96 (2)	95 (1)	93 (1)	94 (1)	95 (2)	95 (1)	94 (1)	90 (1)	90 (2)	86 (2)	88 (2)	89 (2)	87 (5)	82 (3)	71 (4)	84 (3)	80 (4)
Assessments	62 (5)	65 (4)	52 (4)	51 (4)	58 (4)	53 (6)	81 (3)	80 (3)	82 (3)	77 (2)	78 (3)	80 (3)	88 (2)	85 (4)	87 (3)	86 (3)	85 (3)	85 (4)
Science teachers																		
Standards	84 (7)	78 (16)	87 (4)	95 (4)	84 (5)	100 (0)	95 (1)	95 (1)	87 (2)	90 (3)	84 (2)	91 (2)	NA[a]	NA	NA	NA	NA	NA
Assessments	42 (6)	60 (9)	60 (7)	64 (9)	46 (6)	71 (11)	82 (2)	79 (2)	80 (3)	81 (3)	77 (4)	78 (3)	NA	NA	NA	NA	NA	NA

NOTES: Response options included strongly disagree, disagree, agree, and strongly agree. Percentages represent the sum of the agree and strongly agree responses.

[a] Excludes Pennsylvania science teachers because Pennsylvania did not administer a science test.

Table B.48

Elementary School Teachers Reporting Changes in Instructional Time from Year to Year

Subject Changed	California, % (SE)									Georgia, % (SE)									Pennsylvania, % (SE)								
	2002–2003 to 2003–2004			2003–2004 to 2004–2005			2004–2005 to 2005–2006			2002–2003 to 2003–2004			2003–2004 to 2004–2005			2004–2005 to 2005–2006			2002–2003 to 2003–2004			2003–2004 to 2004–2005			2004–2005 to 2005–2006		
	−	=	+	−	=	+	−	=	+	−	=	+	−	=	+	−	=	+	−	=	+	−	=	+	−	=	+
Math	3 (1)	65 (4)	30 (5)	5 (2)	62 (3)	28 (3)	4 (1)	71 (4)	19 (3)	8 (2)	64 (4)	23 (3)	6 (1)	60 (3)	22 (2)	6 (1)	68 (3)	18 (2)	4 (1)	60 (5)	35 (5)	3 (1)	55 (5)	38 (5)	4 (1)	65 (4)	26 (3)
Science	16 (4)	62 (4)	19 (3)	19 (3)	53 (4)	21 (3)	19 (3)	60 (6)	15 (3)	15 (2)	67 (3)	11 (2)	10 (1)	63 (3)	11 (2)	12 (2)	67 (2)	9 (2)	24 (4)	63 (4)	7 (2)	22 (4)	62 (4)	8 (2)	18 (3)	61 (3)	11 (3)
Reading/ ELA	2 (1)	64 (4)	31 (4)	3 (1)	59 (4)	32 (4)	3 (1)	59 (6)	31 (6)	7 (2)	62 (3)	25 (3)	4 (1)	62 (3)	21 (2)	4 (1)	63 (3)	21 (3)	2 (1)	61 (3)	33 (3)	7 (3)	63 (4)	24 (3)	3 (1)	66 (3)	23 (3)
Social Studies	20 (4)	67 (4)	4 (4)	28 (5)	55 (4)	10 (2)	23 (4)	62 (5)	9 (2)	14 (2)	64 (3)	13 (2)	11 (1)	65 (3)	9 (2)	11 (2)	67 (2)	9 (2)	26 (4)	63 (4)	6 (2)	25 (4)	60 (4)	6 (1)	22 (3)	61 (3)	6 (1)
Arts/ Music	26 (5)	58 (7)	11 (4)	23 (4)	60 (4)	9 (2)	23 (4)	61 (5)	9 (2)	18 (3)	68 (4)	5 (1)	9 (2)	69 (3)	4 (1)	6 (2)	70 (3)	8 (2)	3 (1)	91 (2)	1 (0)	2 (1)	88 (2)	3 (1)	1 (1)	89 (1)	1 (0)
PE	16 (4)	70 (5)	8 (3)	23 (4)	58 (5)	11 (3)	15 (3)	70 (5)	9 (2)	9 (2)	78 (3)	5 (2)	5 (1)	74 (2)	5 (1)	6 (2)	77 (2)	4 (1)	3 (1)	91 (2)	1 (0)	3 (1)	88 (2)	3 (1)	2 (2)	86 (2)	3 (1)

NOTES: Response options included decreased by >45 minutes per week, decreased by 1–45 minutes per week, stayed the same, increased by 1–45 minutes per week, increased by >45 minutes per week, and don't know. Percentages for − columns represent the sums of decreased by >45 minutes per week and decreased by 1–45 minutes per week responses. Percentages for + columns represent the sums of increased by >45 minutes per week and increased by 1–45 minutes per week responses. Percentages for = columns represent stayed the same responses. The omitted category is "don't know." PE = physical education.

Table B.49
Middle School Teachers Reporting Changes in Instructional Time from Year to Year

Subject Changed	California, % (SE)									Georgia, % (SE)									Pennsylvania, % (SE)								
	2002–2003 to 2003–2004			2003–2004 to 2004–2005			2004–2005 to 2005–2006			2002–2003 to 2003–2004			2003–2004 to 2004–2005			2004–2005 to 2005–2006			2002–2003 to 2003–2004			2003–2004 to 2004–2005			2004–2005 to 2005–2006		
	–	=	+	–	=	+	–	=	+	–	=	+	–	=	+	–	=	+	–	=	+	–	=	+	–	=	+
Math	3 (1)	67 (5)	17 (4)	1 (0)	67 (3)	20 (3)	2 (1)	73 (3)	11 (3)	4 (1)	64 (3)	19 (3)	5 (2)	53 (5)	29 (6)	4 (1)	62 (4)	19 (4)	3 (2)	70 (5)	19 (4)	2 (1)	78 (5)	14 (4)	2 (1)	69 (3)	18 (4)
Science	6 (2)	60 (5)	8 (2)	9 (3)	63 (4)	10 (3)	9 (5)	66 (4)	6 (3)	6 (1)	65 (3)	14 (2)	5 (1)	51 (4)	23 (5)	7 (2)	62 (4)	14 (3)	7 (2)	73 (5)	11 (4)	7 (2)	77 (6)	6 (3)	4 (2)	70 (5)	12 (6)
Reading/ ELA	2 (1)	60 (5)	11 (3)	3 (1)	60 (4)	14 (3)	2 (1)	59 (3)	13 (5)	3 (1)	61 (3)	19 (3)	8 (2)	48 (4)	23 (5)	5 (2)	54 (4)	19 (3)	1 (0)	64 (5)	21 (6)	3 (1)	74 (6)	9 (3)	3 (1)	62 (5)	13 (3)
Social Studies	6 (3)	58 (4)	5 (2)	13 (5)	59 (4)	5 (1)	10 (5)	60 (3)	2 (1)	4 (1)	61 (3)	12 (2)	5 (1)	51 (4)	20 (5)	6 (1)	59 (4)	12 (3)	3 (1)	71 (3)	10 (4)	9 (3)	75 (6)	3 (1)	7 (3)	65 (5)	6 (2)
Arts/ Music	12 (3)	46 (4)	3 (1)	14 (3)	48 (4)	8 (4)	6 (3)	56 (3)	1 (1)	6 (1)	57 (3)	4 (1)	9 (2)	52 (3)	5 (2)	6 (2)	55 (4)	7 (2)	5 (2)	67 (3)	3 (2)	5 (2)	74 (4)	6 (2)	4 (1)	69 (6)	3 (2)
PE	5 (2)	62 (4)	5 (3)	5 (2)	68 (4)	3 (1)	2 (1)	67 (4)	6 (3)	6 (1)	59 (3)	4 (1)	8 (2)	55 (4)	5 (2)	7 (2)	59 (4)	4 (1)	4 (2)	69 (3)	3 (2)	3 (1)	75 (4)	5 (2)	6 (2)	68 (6)	1 (1)

NOTES: Response options included decreased by >45 minutes per week, decreased by 1–45 minutes per week, stayed the same, increased by 1–45 minutes per week, increased by >45 minutes per week, and don't know. Percentages for – columns represent the sums of decreased by >45 minutes per week and decreased by 1–45 minutes per week responses. Percentages for + columns represent the sums of increased by >45 minutes per week and increased by 1–45 minutes per week responses. Percentages for = columns represent stayed the same responses. The omitted category is "don't know."

Table B.50
Elementary School Mathematics Teachers Reporting That They Use Certain Instructional Techniques

Technique	California, % (SE)		Georgia, % (SE)		Pennsylvania, % (SE)	
	2005	2006	2005	2006	2005	2006
Assign math homework	97 (1)	99 (1)	96 (1)	97 (1)	98 (1)	98 (1)
Have students work on extended math investigations or projects	45 (4)	45 (4)	46 (3)	52 (3)	43 (3)	52 (3)
Introduce content through formal presentations or direct instruction	98 (1)	97 (1)	98 (1)	97 (1)	98 (1)	96 (1)
Provide help to individual students outside of class time	68 (3)	71 (3)	70 (3)	67 (3)	72 (4)	71 (4)
Confer with another teacher about alternative ways to present specific topics or lessons	81 (3)	86 (3)	90 (1)	92 (1)	89 (2)	88 (2)
Have students help other students learn math content	91 (2)	89 (2)	93 (1)	93 (1)	92 (1)	90 (1)
Refer students for extra help outside the classroom	57 (4)	49 (3)	65 (4)	63 (4)	54 (4)	52 (4)
Plan different assignments based on performance	82 (2)	80 (3)	90 (1)	87 (2)	81 (2)	79 (3)
Reteach topics because performance on assignments or assessments did not meet expectations	93 (2)	97 (1)	96 (1)	98 (1)	89 (2)	95 (1)
Review assessment results to identify individual students who need supplemental instruction	91 (2)	94 (2)	95 (1)	96 (1)	89 (1)	93 (1)
Review assessment results to identify topics requiring more or less emphasis in instruction	90 (2)	93 (2)	94 (1)	96 (1)	87 (1)	91 (1)
Conduct a preassessment to find out what students know about a topic	65 (4)	67 (3)	67 (3)	76 (3)	60 (5)	58 (3)

NOTES: Response options were never, rarely (a few times a year), sometimes (once or twice a month), and often (once a week or more). Percentages represent the sum of the sometimes and often responses.

Table B.51
Middle School Mathematics Teachers Reporting That They Use Certain Instructional Techniques

Technique	California, % (SE)		Georgia, % (SE)		Pennsylvania, % (SE)	
	2005	2006	2005	2006	2005	2006
Assign math homework	94 (2)	98 (1)	92 (2)	90 (2)	94 (2)	95 (2)
Have students work on extended math investigations or projects	28 (4)	34 (4)	39 (3)	42 (3)	26 (3)	39 (6)
Introduce content through formal presentations or direct instruction	95 (2)	98 (1)	97 (1)	98 (1)	99 (0)	98 (1)
Provide help to individual students outside of class time	85 (4)	87 (3)	85 (2)	86 (2)	80 (11)	76 (6)
Confer with another teacher about alternative ways to present specific topics or lessons	81 (3)	79 (5)	84 (2)	91 (2)	72 (10)	81 (3)
Have students help other students learn math content	86 (2)	87 (2)	94 (1)	95 (1)	84 (4)	86 (3)
Refer students for extra help outside the classroom	70 (3)	73 (6)	63 (4)	68 (3)	66 (4)	64 (4)
Plan different assignments based on performance	68 (2)	67 (5)	81 (2)	83 (2)	69 (5)	73 (5)
Reteach topics because performance on assignments or assessments did not meet expectations	95 (2)	97 (1)	93 (1)	95 (1)	87 (3)	90 (3)
Review assessment results to identify individual students who need supplemental instruction	84 (3)	91 (3)	89 (2)	91 (1)	75 (6)	80 (5)
Review assessment results to identify topics requiring more or less emphasis in instruction	86 (2)	86 (2)	90 (2)	95 (1)	83 (4)	81 (5)
Conduct a preassessment to find out what students know about a topic	49 (4)	51 (5)	65 (3)	68 (3)	41 (9)	56 (10)

NOTES: Response options were never, rarely (a few times a year), sometimes (once or twice a month), and often (once a week or more). Percentages represent the sum of the sometimes and often responses.

Table B.52
Elementary School Science Teachers Reporting That They Use Certain Instructional Techniques

Technique	California, % (SE)		Georgia, % (SE)		Pennsylvania, % (SE)	
	2005	2006	2005	2006	2005	2006
Assign science homework	51 (4)	44 (6)	75 (3)	73 (3)	57 (4)	56 (4)
Have students do hands-on laboratory science activities or investigations	72 (3)	71 (5)	81 (2)	85 (3)	84 (3)	87 (2)
Introduce content through formal presentations or direct instruction	93 (2)	92 (2)	99 (0)	99 (1)	97 (1)	95 (1)
Provide help to individual students outside of class time	25 (3)	26 (4)	41 (3)	37 (3)	30 (3)	30 (3)
Confer with another teacher about alternative ways to present specific topics or lessons	62 (5)	64 (5)	83 (2)	84 (2)	68 (4)	66 (4)
Have students help other students learn science content	66 (3)	64 (4)	87 (2)	84 (2)	75 (3)	73 (3)
Refer students for extra help outside the classroom	20 (3)	18 (3)	35 (3)	28 (3)	16 (3)	13 (2)
Plan different assignments or lessons based on performance	38 (3)	36 (4)	64 (4)	59 (3)	37 (3)	40 (3)
Reteach topics because performance on assignments or assessments did not meet expectations	57 (4)	58 (5)	81 (3)	80 (3)	54 (4)	58 (3)
Review assessment results to identify individual students who need supplemental instruction	61 (4)	62 (5)	81 (2)	83 (2)	62 (3)	68 (3)
Review assessment results to identify topics requiring more or less emphasis in instruction	61 (4)	63 (5)	82 (2)	82 (2)	60 (3)	66 (3)
Conduct a preassessment to find out what students know about a topic	42 (4)	39 (5)	53 (3)	55 (3)	43 (4)	44 (4)

NOTES: Response options were never, rarely (a few times a year), sometimes (once or twice a month), and often (once a week or more). Percentages represent the sum of the sometimes and often responses

Table B.53
Middle School Science Teachers Reporting That They Use Certain Instructional Techniques

Technique	California, % (SE)		Georgia, % (SE)		Pennsylvania, % (SE)	
	2005	2006	2005	2006	2005	2006
Assign science homework	75 (7)	69 (8)	87 (3)	83 (3)	78 (6)	78 (5)
Have students do hands-on laboratory science activities or investigations	82 (5)	78 (9)	85 (2)	84 (3)	76 (6)	87 (4)
Introduce content through formal presentations or direct instruction	98 (1)	93 (4)	98 (1)	97 (1)	94 (4)	97 (1)
Provide help to individual students outside of class time	65 (7)	64 (9)	76 (3)	72 (3)	56 (10)	68 (8)
Confer with another teacher about alternative ways to present specific topics or lessons	69 (5)	67 (9)	84 (2)	89 (2)	69 (6)	78 (5)
Have students help other students learn science content	80 (4)	68 (5)	90 (2)	90 (2)	74 (6)	79 (4)
Refer students for extra help outside the classroom	43 (5)	25 (5)	57 (3)	53 (3)	39 (7)	38 (6)
Plan different assignments or lessons based on performance	46 (7)	40 (5)	74 (3)	76 (3)	65 (5)	66 (4)
Reteach topics because performance on assignments or assessments did not meet expectations	59 (5)	63 (7)	80 (2)	82 (3)	62 (3)	71 (4)
Review assessment results to identify individual students who need supplemental instruction	66 (7)	60 (7)	80 (3)	87 (2)	79 (6)	79 (4)
Review assessment results to identify topics requiring more or less emphasis in instruction	70 (5)	55 (9)	85 (2)	88 (2)	76 (3)	78 (3)
Conduct a preassessment to find out what students know about a topic	53 (5)	37 (5)	63 (3)	69 (4)	65 (3)	53 (6)

NOTES: Response options were never, rarely (a few times a year), sometimes (once or twice a month), and often (once a week or more). Percentages represent the sum of the sometimes and often responses.

Table B.54
Teachers Agreeing with Statements About the State's Accountability System

Statement	California, % (SE)						Georgia, % (SE)						Pennsylvania, % (SE)					
	2004		2005		2006		2004		2005		2006		2004		2005		2006	
	Elem	Mid	Elem	Mid	Elem	Mid	Elem	Mid	Elem	Mid	Elem	Mid	Elem	Mid	Elem	Mid	Elem	Mid
The state's accountability system leaves little time to teach content not on the state tests	82 (4)	86 (2)	89 (2)	90 (2)	89 (2)	88 (3)	82 (2)	84 (2)	87 (1)	85 (2)	82 (2)	83 (2)	87 (3)	87 (2)	88 (2)	87 (2)	87 (2)	95 (2)
As a result of the state's accountability system, high-achieving students are not receiving appropriately challenging curriculum or instruction[a]			52 (3)	47 (3)	52 (4)	54 (3)			49 (2)	55 (2)	46 (3)	51 (2)			39 (4)	52 (6)	46 (3)	56 (5)

NOTES: Response options included strongly disagree, disagree, agree, and strongly agree. Percentages represent the sum of the agree and strongly agree responses.

[a] Blank cells indicate that we did not ask this question in 2004.

Table B.55
Administrators Reporting Inadequate Fiscal or Physical Capital as a Hindrance to Their Improvement Efforts

Hindrance	California, % (SE)									Georgia, % (SE)									Pennsylvania, % (SE)								
	2004			2005			2006			2004			2005			2006			2004			2005			2006		
	E	M	S	E	M	S	E	M	S	E	M	S	E	M	S	E	M	S	E	M	S	E	M	S	E	M	S
Lack of adequate funding	67 (11)	71 (10)	84 (2)	81 (7)	80 (8)	98 (9)	55 (10)	74 (10)	81 (9)	73 (7)	77 (6)	81 (1)	43 (7)	67 (8)	99 (11)	44 (7)	60 (9)	93 (5)	64 (8)	75 (10)	80 (1)	66 (9)	72 (10)	98 (10)	55	74	86
Inadequate school facilities	9 (6)	30 (14)	27 (6)	3 (2)	8 (5)	10 (14)	11 (6)	23 (8)	8 (6)	23 (8)	29 (8)	30 (12)	23 (7)	18 (7)	19 (13)	11 (4)	12 (5)	4 (3)	23 (7)	30 (11)	31 (12)	16 (6)	30 (11)	26 (11)	14	38	17
Shortage of standards-based curriculum materials			34 (9)			14 (14)			16 (9)			31 (14)			46 (12)			40 (13)			30 (13)			34			32
Unanticipated problems with space, facilities, and trans-portation				29 (9)	21 (7)		33 (8)	14 (5)					18 (5)	15 (5)		24 (7)	13 (5)					23 (7)	20 (9)		18	38	

NOTES: Response options included not a hindrance, a minor hindrance, a moderate hindrance, and a great hindrance. Percentages represent the sum of the moderate and great hindrance responses. "E" is elementary principal, "M" is middle school principal, and "S" is superintendent.

Table B.56
Teachers Reporting Inadequate Resources as a Hindrance to Students' Academic Success

	California, % (SE)						Georgia, % (SE)						Pennsylvania, % (SE)					
	2004		2005		2006		2004		2005		2006		2004		2005		2006	
Hindrance	Elem	Mid	Elem	Mid	Elem	Mid	Elem	Mid	Elem	Mid	Elem	Mid	Elem	Mid	Elem	Mid	Elem	Mid
Large class size	51 (4)	66 (4)	59 (4)	69 (4)	55 (7)	60 (4)	44 (3)	54 (4)	39 (3)	57 (3)	40 (3)	55 (4)	55 (3)	60 (4)	47 (4)	57 (4)	47 (3)	50 (5)
Inadequate instructional resources (e.g., textbooks, equipment)	26 (6)	38 (4)	33 (3)	34 (3)	27 (4)	26 (4)	25 (3)	31 (3)	28 (3)	35 (3)	26 (3)	36 (3)	26 (4)	23 (4)	33 (4)	33 (6)	32 (3)	27 (3)
Lack of school resources to provide the extra help for students who need it	41 (7)	48 (5)	42 (5)	37 (4)	41 (4)	30 (5)	20 (3)	37 (3)	23 (3)	34 (3)	22 (3)	31 (3)	33 (4)	32 (4)	32 (4)	31 (6)	34 (4)	33 (3)

NOTES: Response options included not a hindrance, a minor hindrance, a moderate hindrance, and a great hindrance. Percentages represent the sum of the moderate and great hindrance responses.

Table B.57
Administrators Reporting Inadequate Human Capital as a Hindrance to Their Improvement Efforts

Hindrance	California, % (SE)									Georgia, % (SE)									Pennsylvania, % (SE)								
	2004			2005			2006			2004			2005			2006			2004			2005			2006		
	E	M	S	E	M	S	E	M	S	E	M	S	E	M	S	E	M	S	E	M	S	E	M	S	E	M	S
Shortage of qualified principals			15 (8)			22 (11)			25 (10)			26 (13)			36 (13)			38 (12)			30 (11)			29 (13)			18 (11)
Shortage of highly qualified teachers	29 (9)	35 (9)		12 (5)	39 (10)		24 (8)	25 (9)		18 (7)	21 (4)		7 (4)	32 (8)		13 (5)	28 (6)		9 (6)	18 (8)		10 (5)	25 (11)		8	19	
Shortage of highly qualified *math* teachers						40 (12)			76 (10)						69 (13)			66 (14)						33			28
Shortage of highly qualified *science* teachers						43 (13)			60 (11)						69 (13)			78 (12)						28			39
Shortage of highly qualified teacher aides and para-professionals	38 (12)	23 (8)		22 (8)	28 (9)		31 (10)	24 (9)		14 (5)	11 (4)		9 (5)	8 (5)		20 (7)	12 (5)		16 (7)	17 (7)		27 (8)	34 (11)		25	19	
Teacher turnover	22 (10)	19 (7)		20 (9)	12 (6)		19 (9)	10 (7)		19 (6)	20 (6)		15 (6)	25 (9)		19 (7)	24 (7)		2 (1)	33 (14)		13 (5)	21 (10)		9	18	

Table B.57—Continued

Hindrance	California, % (SE)									Georgia, % (SE)									Pennsylvania, % (SE)								
	2004			2005			2006			2004			2005			2006			2004			2005			2006		
	E	M	S	E	M	S	E	M	S	E	M	S	E	M	S	E	M	S	E	M	S	E	M	S	E	M	S
Shortage/lack of high-quality PD opportunities for *teachers*	31 (11)	34 (13)	48 (14)	32 (10)	38 (10)	47 (13)	42 (11)	44 (10)	42 (11)	25 (7)	11 (5)	26 (11)	16 (5)	17 (6)	45 (14)	16 (6)	18 (6)	30 (12)	16 (6)	51 (13)	30 (11)	22 (9)	19	39	32	49	51
Shortage/lack of high-quality PD opportunities for *principals*	44 (15)	30 (11)	39 (13)	29 (8)	39 (10)	37 (12)	29 (11)	47 (13)	40 (12)	22 (7)	12 (5)	29 (13)	10 (5)	10 (4)	45 (14)	11 (6)	12 (5)	16 (8)	16 (6)	38 (13)	42 (12)	34 (9)	22	51	36	43	52
Insufficient staff time to meet administrative responsibilities				71 (7)	72 (12)		57 (9)	69 (10)					56 (6)	43 (8)		62 (7)	65 (9)					55 (10)	63		58	38	

NOTES: Response options included not a hindrance, a minor hindrance, a moderate hindrance, and a great hindrance. Percentages represent the sum of the moderate and great hindrance responses. "E" is elementary principal, "M" is middle school principal, and "S" is superintendent.

Table B.58
Teachers Reporting Inadequate Time as a Hindrance to Students' Academic Success

Hindrance	California, % (SE)						Georgia, % (SE)						Pennsylvania, % (SE)					
	2004		2005		2006		2004		2005		2006		2004		2005		2006	
	Elem	Mid	Elem	Mid	Elem	Mid	Elem	Mid	Elem	Mid	Elem	Mid	Elem	Mid	Elem	Mid	Elem	Mid
Insufficient class time to cover all the curriculum	71 (3)	56 (4)	70 (3)	61 (5)	75 (3)	60 (4)	58 (2)	49 (4)	59 (2)	46 (2)	58 (2)	40 (3)	58 (4)	49 (3)	64 (3)	47 (6)	64 (4)	54 (4)
Lack of teacher planning time built into the school day[a]			62 (3)	43 (4)	63 (4)	37 (6)			44 (3)	38 (3)	42 (4)	32 (4)			52 (3)	29 (6)	53 (4)	30 (4)

NOTES: Response options included not a hindrance, a minor hindrance, a moderate hindrance, and a great hindrance. Percentages represent the sum of the moderate and great hindrance responses.

[a] Blank cells indicate that we did not ask this question in 2004.

Table B.59
Administrators Reporting Inadequate Time as a Moderate or Great Hindrance to Their Improvement Efforts

Hindrance	California, % (SE)									Georgia, % (SE)									Pennsylvania, % (SE)								
	2004			2005			2006			2004			2005			2006			2004			2005			2006		
	E	M	S	E	M	S	E	M	S	E	M	S	E	M	S	E	M	S	E	M	S	E	M	S	E	M	S
Inadequate lead time to prepare before implementing reforms	57 (12)	56 (10)	92 (5)	46 (9)	31 (10)	85 (7)	36 (9)	38 (10)	58 (11)	67 (9)	41 (8)	86 (7)	34 (7)	36 (10)	69 (13)	43 (8)	40 (9)	32 (10)	52 (10)	47 (12)	64 (12)	34 (7)	33 (12)	57 (15)	22	64	73
Lack of teacher planning time built into the school day				71 (9)	36 (10)		56 (6)	40 (12)					44 (6)	22 (7)		39 (8)	17 (6)					41 (8)	12 (8)		37	20	

NOTES: Response options included not a hindrance, a minor hindrance, a moderate hindrance, and a great hindrance. Percentages represent the sum of the moderate and great hindrance responses. "E" is elementary principal, "M" is middle school principal, and "S" is superintendent.

Table B.60
Teachers Reporting Student Background Conditions as a Hindrance to Students' Academic Success

Hindrance	California, % (SE)						Georgia, % (SE)						Pennsylvania, % (SE)					
	2004		2005		2006		2004		2005		2006		2004		2005		2006	
	Elem	Mid	Elem	Mid	Elem	Mid	Elem	Mid	Elem	Mid	Elem	Mid	Elem	Mid	Elem	Mid	Elem	Mid
Inadequate basic skills or prior preparation	70 (6)	79 (6)	78 (5)	83 (3)	75 (3)	84 (3)	71 (5)	85 (2)	70 (4)	86 (2)	66 (4)	83 (2)	62 (5)	81 (4)	66 (5)	85 (2)	65 (4)	83 (3)
Lack of support from parents	68 (6)	78 (6)	75 (5)	80 (4)	72 (6)	80 (4)	74 (5)	85 (2)	75 (5)	86 (2)	73 (5)	83 (2)	72 (5)	79 (4)	69 (5)	85 (2)	72 (4)	85 (3)
Student absenteeism and tardiness	51 (6)	68 (6)	61 (5)	70 (4)	64 (6)	73 (5)	54 (5)	76 (3)	51 (4)	74 (2)	47 (4)	69 (2)	52 (5)	71 (3)	51 (5)	82 (5)	51 (4)	71 (4)
Wide range of student abilities to address in class	80 (4)	68 (5)	82 (3)	77 (3)	76 (4)	77 (4)	67 (3)	69 (2)	65 (3)	71 (2)	65 (3)	69 (2)	76 (3)	72 (3)	78 (3)	75 (4)	73 (3)	72 (3)

NOTES: Response options included not a hindrance, a minor hindrance, a moderate hindrance, and a great hindrance. Percentages represent the sum of the moderate and great hindrance responses.

Table B.61
Superintendents Reporting That Their Districts Have Sufficient Staff with Necessary Skills in Certain Areas

Skill	California, % (SE)			Georgia, % (SE)			Pennsylvania, % (SE)		
	2004	2005	2006	2004	2005	2006	2004	2005	2006
Facilitate improvements in low-performing schools	61 (14)	62 (14)	79 (9)	74 (12)	67 (13)	65 (12)	80 (10)	32 (15)	44 (14)
Help schools to analyze data for school improvement	70 (14)	68 (12)	74 (10)	68 (13)	66 (14)	80 (10)	86 (8)	55 (16)	31 (12)
Help schools identify research-based strategies for improvement	70 (14)	57 (12)	72 (10)	71 (12)	73 (13)	77 (11)	92 (5)	58 (16)	38 (14)
Conduct PD tailored to the needs of teachers	52 (14)	35 (11)	57 (11)	31 (11)	68 (14)	62 (12)	73 (11)	74 (13)	34 (13)
Conduct PD tailored to the needs of principals	65 (14)	27 (10)	58 (11)	34 (11)	64 (14)	68 (12)	65 (12)	48 (16)	31 (12)
Align curriculum with state content standards and state assessments	94 (5)	52 (11)	69 (10)	63 (12)	70 (13)	70 (11)	88 (8)	85 (10)	38 (13)

NOTE: Response options included yes and no.

Table B.62
Administrators Reporting Frequent Changes in Policy or Leadership as a Hindrance to Their Improvement Efforts

| | California, % (SE) | | | | | | | | | Georgia, % (SE) | | | | | | | | | Pennsylvania, % (SE) | | | | | | | | |
| | 2004 | | | 2005 | | | 2006 | | | 2004 | | | 2005 | | | 2006 | | | 2004 | | | 2005 | | | 2006 | | |
Hindrance	E	M	S	E	M	S	E	M	S	E	M	S	E	M	S	E	M	S	E	M	S	E	M	S	E	M	S
Frequent changes in state policy or leadership			87 (8)			71 (12)			71 (11)			76 (12)			79 (12)			67 (12)			73 (11)			98 (1)			68 (13)
Frequent changes in district policy and priorities	22 (7)	24 (10)		46 (10)	15 (5)		37 (12)	11 (5)		21 (7)	28 (7)		11 (4)	18 (6)		15 (4)	27 (10)		21 (6)	30 (9)		19 (7)	15 (7)		19	32	
Frequent changes in district leadership	12 (9)	13 (11)		30 (10)	20 (8)		29 (13)	10 (6)		18 (7)	20 (7)		14 (4)	10 (4)		11 (5)	16 (7)		9 (5)	23 (9)		14 (6)	9 (7)		13	25	
Complying with teacher association rules/ policies			73 (12)			71 (12)			59 (11)			0 (NA)			7 (6)			12 (9)			42 (12)			51			70
Disagreements with district school board over policies			11 (8)			2 (2)			2 (2)			13 (13)			17 (9)			33 (13)			9 (9)			21			23

NOTES: Response options included not a hindrance, a minor hindrance, a moderate hindrance, and a great hindrance. Percentages represent the sum of the moderate and great hindrance responses. "E" is elementary principal, "M" is middle school principal, and "S" is superintendent.

Table B.63
Principals Reporting Lack of Guidance for Teaching Standards to Students Subgroups as a Hindrance to Their School Improvement Efforts

| Hindrance | California, % (SE) | | | | Georgia, % (SE) | | | | Pennsylvania, % (SE) | | | |
| | 2005 | | 2006 | | 2005 | | 2006 | | 2005 | | 2006 | |
	Elem	Mid	Elem	Mid	Elem	Mid	Elem	Mid	Elem	Mid	Elem	Mid
Lack of guidance for teaching grade-level standards to special education students)	51 (10)	26 (9)	39 (9)	37 (9)	17 (6)	21 (8)	28 (8)	39 (10)	27 (8)	41 (14)	23 (7)	21 (9)
Lack of guidance for teaching grade-level standards to ELLs	47 (10)	15 (7)	49 (10)	45 (11)	19 (7)	21 (6)	22 (9)	30 (7)	27 (8)	8 (3)	18 (5)	20 (7)

NOTES: Response options included not a hindrance, a minor hindrance, a moderate hindrance, and a great hindrance. Percentages represent the sum of the moderate and great hindrance responses.

Bibliography

20 U.S. Code § 6311–6322, Education: Strengthening and Improvement of Elementary and Secondary Schools: Improving the Academic Achievement of the Disadvantaged: Improving Basic Programs Operated by Local Educational Agencies: Basic Program Requirements, January 2, 2006.

California Department of Education, Guidelines on Academic Preparation for State Assessments, Sacramento, Calif.: California Department of Education, April 2004. As of July 14, 2008:
http://www.cde.ca.gov/ta/tg/sa/documents/academicprep.pdf

————, Public Schools Accountability Act (PSAA), Sacramento, Calif.: California Department of Education, last reviewed May 14, 2008. As of July 14, 2008:
http://www.cde.ca.gov/ta/ac/pa/

California State Board of Education, Content Standards, Sacramento, Calif.: California State Board of Education, last reviewed June 27, 2008. As of July 14, 2008:
http://www.cde.ca.gov/be/st/ss/

Center on Education Policy (CEP), *From the Capital to the Classroom: Year 4 of the No Child Left Behind Act,* Washington, D.C., March 2006.

————, *Educational Architects: Do State Education Agencies Have the Tools Necessary to Implement NCLB?* Washington D.C., May 2007a.

————, *Moving Beyond Identification: Assisting Schools in Improvement,* Washington D.C., July 2007b.

————, *Managing More Than a Thousand Remodeling Projects: School Restructuring in California,* Washington D.C., February 2008.

Cronin, John, Michael Dahlin, Deborah Adkins, and G. Gage Kingsbury, *The Proficiency Illusion,* Washington, D.C.: Thomas B. Fordham Institute, October 4, 2007. As of July 14, 2008:
http://www.edexcellence.net/detail/news.cfm?news_id=376

Finn, Chester E., Jr., Michael J. Petrilli, and Liam Julian, *The State of State Standards 2006,* Washington, D.C.: Thomas B. Fordham Foundation, August 29, 2006. As of July 14, 2008:
http://www.edexcellence.net/detail/news.cfm?news_id=358

Georgia Department of Education, Curriculum Frequently Asked Questions, Atlanta, Ga.: Georgia Department of Education, undated. As of July 14, 2008:
http://www.georgiastandards.org/faqs.aspx

Hamilton, Laura S., Brian M. Stecher, Julie A. Marsh, Jennifer Sloan McCombs, Abby Robyn, Jennifer Russell, Scott Naftel, and Heather Barney, *Standards-Based Accountability Under No Child Left Behind: Experiences of Teachers and Administrators in Three States,* Santa Monica, Calif.: RAND Corporation, MG-589-NSF, 2007. As of July 14, 2008:
http://www.rand.org/pubs/monographs/MG589/

Harr, Jenifer J., Tom Parrish, Miguel Socias, and Paul Gubbins, *Evaluation Study of California's High Priority Schools Grant Program: Final Report*, Washington, D.C.: American Institutes for Research, September 9, 2007. As of July 14, 2008:
http://eric.ed.gov/ERICWebPortal/custom/portlets/recordDetails/detailmini.
jsp?_nfpb=true&_&ERICExtSearch_SearchValue_0=ED499197&ERICExtSearc
h_SearchType_0=no&accno=ED499197

Marsh, Julie A., John F. Pane, and Laura S. Hamilton, *Making Sense of Data-Driven Decision Making in Education: Evidence from Recent RAND Research,* Santa Monica, Calif.: RAND Corporation, OP-170-EDU, 2006. As of July 14, 2008:
http://www.rand.org/pubs/occasional_papers/OP170/

National Center for Education Statistics (NCES), Common Core of Data, *Build a Table,* Washington, D.C.: U.S. Department of Education, undated. As of July 14, 2008:
http://nces.ed.gov/ccd/bat/

———, *Mapping 2005 State Proficiency Standards Onto the NAEP Scales,* Washington, D.C.: U.S. Department of Education, NCES 2007-482, June 2007. As of July 14, 2008:
http://nces.ed.gov/nationsreportcard/pubs/studies/2007482.asp

O'Connell, Jack, *A California Perspective on Growth Models and Adequate Yearly Progress (AYP),* written testimony submitted to the Aspen Institute—Commission on No Child Left Behind, May 22, 2006. As of July 14, 2008:
http://www.cde.ca.gov/nr/sp/yr06/yr06sp0522.asp

Pennsylvania Department of Education, "English as a Second Language Program Statistics," Harrisburg, Pa.: Pennsylvania Department of Education, content last modified on October 30, 2006. As of July 14, 2008:
http://www.pde.state.pa.us/esl/cwp/view.asp?a=3&Q=70150

P.L. 107-110, *No Child Left Behind Act of 2001,* January 8, 2002.

Poston, William, et al., *Preliminary Evaluation of Curriculum Development and Design in Reading and Language Arts, Mathematics, Social Studies, and Science: A Preliminary External Curriculum Audit of the Georgia Performance Standards (Preliminary Draft),* Bloomington, Ind.: International Curriculum Management Audit Center, Phi Delta Kappa International, April 23, 2004. As of July 29, 2008:
http://www.gpee.org/Curriculum-Audit.49.0.html

U.S. Department of Education, *State and Local Implementation of the No Child Left Behind Act, Volume II—Teacher Quality Under NCLB: Interim Report,* Washington, D.C., 2007a.

———, *State and Local Implementation of the No Child Left Behind Act, Volume III—Accountability Under NCLB: Interim Report,* Washington, D.C., 2007b.